From the Library of

CALDWELL COLLEGE

Caldwell, New Jersey 07006

CALDWELL COLLEGE LIBRARY
CALDWELL, NEW JERSEY 07006

FILM FOCUS

Ronald Gottesman and Harry M. Geduld
General Editors

The Film Focus series presents the best that has been written about the art of film and the men who created it. Combining criticism with history, biography, and analysis of technique, the volumes in the series explore the many dimensions of the film medium and its impact on modern society.

Ronald Gottesman is Associate Professor of English at Livingston College of Rutgers University. He has written numerous books on film, editing and such authors and directors as Sinclair and Eisenstein.

FOCUS ON
CITIZEN KANE

edited by
RONALD GOTTESMAN

Prentice-Hall, Inc.
Englewood Cliffs, N.J.

CALDWELL COLLEGE LIBRARY
CALDWELL, NEW JERSEY 07006

*Illustrations courtesy Gene Andrewski
and the Museum of Modern Art/Film Stills Archive.*

Copyright © 1971 by RONALD GOTTESMAN

A SPECTRUM BOOK

*All rights reserved.
No part of this book may be reproduced in any form
or by any means without permission in writing
from the publisher.*

C–13-134759-4
P–13-134742-X
Library of Congress Catalog Card Number 74–153434

Printed in the United States of America.

Current printing (last number):
10   9   8   7   6   5   4   3   2   1

PRENTICE-HALL INTERNATIONAL, INC. (*London*)
PRENTICE-HALL OF AUSTRALIA, PTY. LTD. (*Sydney*)
PRENTICE-HALL OF CANADA, LTD. (*Toronto*)
PRENTICE-HALL OF INDIA PRIVATE LIMITED (*New Delhi*)
PRENTICE-HALL OF JAPAN, INC. (*Tokyo*)

for
John and Barbara
and
Tracy, Adam, Joshua,
and
Julie

CONTENTS

Preface ix

Citizen Kane: Cast and Credits xi

Introduction: *Citizen Kane:* Past, Present, and Future
 by Ronald Gottesman 1

A Trip to Don Quixoteland: Conversations with Orson Welles
 by Juan Cobos, Miguel Rubio, and J. A. Pruneda 7

Orson Welles: Of Time and Loss
 by William Johnson 25

REVIEWS

John O'Hara 45

Bosley Crowther 47

Otis Ferguson 51

Cedric Belfrage 54

Tangye Lean 59

ESSAYS

"*Citizen Kane* Is Not about Louella Parsons' Boss"
 by Orson Welles 67

Score for a Film
 by Bernard Herrmann 69

How I Broke the Rules in *Citizen Kane*
 by Gregg Toland, A. S. C. 73

Citizen Kane: Background and a Critique
   by Roy A. Fowler   78

Citizen Kane: The American Baroque
   by Andrew Sarris   102

The Study of a Colossus
   by Peter Cowie   109

Citizen Kane Revisited
   by Arthur Knight   120

COMMENTARIES

Jorge Luis Borges: Citizen Kane   127

André Bazin: The Originality of Welles as a Director   128

François Truffaut: Citizen Kane   129

Michael Stephanick: The Most Advanced Film Screened in Class This Year: A Catalogue of Effects   133

Charles Higham: From *The Films of Orson Welles*   137

Letter of Clearance from the Production Code Office   145

   Plot Synopsis   147
   Content Outline   149
   Script Extract   155
   Filmography   169
   Selected Bibliographies   171
   Index   175

PREFACE

Preparation of this volume was expedited by Regina Cornwell, formerly director of the Film Study Center at the Museum of Modern Art, and by the staff of the Lincoln Center branch of the New York Public Library. Judy and Mark Bernheim translated into English material from Italian, French, and German; Mark Bezanson translated several long essays from French. Claudia Wilson oversaw the production of this volume and did so with rare grace and efficiency. David Aronson, Leslie Clark, and Judy Bernheim helped greatly and variously with the research and typing of the manuscript. I am grateful also to three friends who read the manuscript and who made typically perceptive criticisms of it: Harry M. Geduld, Albert J. LaValley, and Gerald Rabkin. They and many other friends, colleagues, and students listened and talked (mostly the former) about *Citizen Kane* during the months the project absorbed my attention. My wife and children, as always, indulged me dreadfully while I was working as well as when I was only pretending to.

CITIZEN KANE
RKO Radio Pictures, 1940–41, A Mercury Production

SCREENPLAY	Herman J. Mankiewicz and Orson Welles (with the assistance of Joseph Cotten and John Houseman)
DIRECTION	Orson Welles
PHOTOGRAPHY	Gregg Toland
EDITING	Robert Wise (and Mark Robson)
ART DIRECTION	Van Nest Polglase and Perry Ferguson
COSTUMES	Edward Stevenson
DECORS	Darrell Silvera
MUSIC	Bernard Herrmann

TIME: 119 MINUTES

Filmed from 30 July to 23 October, 1940 in RKO Studios, Hollywood. Press showing 9 April 1941 in New York and Los Angeles. Premieres: 1 May 1941, Palace Theatre, New York; 8 May 1941, El Capitan Theatre in Hollywood.

CAST

Charles Foster Kane	ORSON WELLES
Jedediah Leland	JOSEPH COTTEN
Susan Alexander Kane	DOROTHY COMINGORE
Kane's mother	AGNES MOOREHEAD
Emily Norton Kane	RUTH WARRICK
James W. Gettys	RAY COLLINS
Mr. Carter	ERSKINE SANFORD
Mr. Bernstein	EVERETT SLOANE
Thompson, the reporter (and *Newsreel Narrator*)	WILLIAM ALLAND
Raymond, the butler	PAUL STEWART
Walter Parks Thatcher	GEORGE COULOURIS
Signor Matisti	FORTUNIO BONANOVA
Headwaiter	GUS SCHILLING
Rawlston	PHILIP VAN ZANDT
Miss Anderson	GEORGIA BACKUS
Kane, Sr.	HARRY SHANNON
Kane's son	SONNY BUPP
Kane at age of eight	BUDDY SWAN
Hillman	RICHARD BAER
Georgia	JOAN BLAIR

Introduction

CITIZEN KANE:
Past, Present, and Future
by RONALD GOTTESMAN

> *"A film is never really good unless the camera is an eye in the head of a poet."*
> —ORSON WELLES

Gertrude Stein observed once that it commonly takes about a generation for the ugliness to wear off a truly revolutionary work of art. Though *Citizen Kane* was widely acclaimed from the beginning and has never quite suffered from neglect or obscurity, much of the early praise was offered for the wrong reasons and the film has suffered more than most at the hands of parochial, ill-informed, and shallow reviewers and commentators. Indeed, with few exceptions, it is only in the past decade that anything like genuine analysis and criticism has begun to acknowledge and to try to come to terms with the heft, complexity, and resonance of this extraordinary act of imagination. This is not to say—as I will presently show in greater detail—that *Citizen Kane* is now fully—or even adequately—accounted for. The film—like its grand, ungodly God-like protagonist—still contains many mysteries. Though we have got beyond its first "No Trespassing" sign, we have not fully explored all the byways of what Jorge Luis Borges characterized as a "centreless labyrinth."

Publicity promotes but by inflating it creates vulnerability, especially if its subject is young and irreverent. So, although Welles's flamboyance on Broadway and his notorious inventiveness on radio earned him his choice of film contracts in 1939, payment would in due course be extracted by the jealous, the suspicious and the malevolent even before the prerelease troubles with columnist Louella Parsons and her boss

William Randolph Hearst—the film's putative subject—insured a mixed reception for *Kane*.

Established reviewers like Howard Barnes, Kate Cameron, Bosley Crowther, and Otis Ferguson in this country and Dilys Powell and William Whitebait in England dealt honestly and responsibly with the film, but when *Kane* had its premiere on May 1, 1941, a phalanx of critical fallacies was unleashed on it. It was variously asserted that Welles was too young to make a good picture, that Kane was too nasty a subject for a moral film, that Welles was too didactic and political, that the film was too subjective, the plot too complicated and the story boring, that the techniques and special effects were eclectic and derivative, that they departed too radically from accepted conventions—and so forth. In the fall, when the film was released in England, the nonsense was quickly internationalized. A happily anonymous reviewer in the *Documentary News Letter* for November 1941 offered the following insight: "Welles was taken from home at an early age and was brought up on culture by intellect. The same thing happened to Kane, and Welles is obviously very sympathetic—he regrets his background, and the whole story of 'Rosebud' is most likely Welles's and not Kane's—Welles seeking his way back to the warm maternal bosom." If Freud had not died a couple of years earlier, such twaddle surely would have brought him low. To read such reviews is to understand the origins of Welles's complaint that reviewers write about Welles rather than about his work.

Obviously not all of the reviews were stupid or venal. But even so influential a cultural force as Jean-Paul Sartre could utter manifestly contradictory and otherwise perverse judgments four years later when the film reached France, seeing the film as an illustration of the rootless and privatistic artist in America trying to win the masses over to liberalism. And some eighteen years after its release François Truffaut, while acknowledging the influence of *Citizen Kane,* reduced it to the status of journalism, arguing curiously that because he remembered the sound track better than the images the picture couldn't be as good as he used to think it was. (André Bazin, Roger Leenhardt, Maurice Bessy, and Jean Cocteau, among many other French critics, one is happy to report, were much more fair to *Kane*.)

The Americans, English and French did not control the world market in critical obtuseness. German criticism of the film, though, is generally more dully pedantic than stupid, while Italian criticism of *Kane* is typically soaringly abstract and overingenious. This is not the place, however, to review the whole body of criticism and commentary that has accumulated over the three decades since *Kane* was released. Let me turn, rather, to what I have selected from this material in order to remind us of those experiments and accomplishments in complex narrative structure, pace, lighting, composition, camera angle, the use of special wide-angle and depth-of-focus lenses, naturalistic sound track, makeup, acting technique, and editing which an omniverous, thoughtful and relentless man in his mid-twenties fashioned into a film peculiarly notable for both its literary and filmic power.

The Cobos, Rubio and Pruneda interview—by far the best one currently in print—is designed to introduce Welles: his personality, his social and moral attitudes, his outlook as a director and some of his own feelings about *Citizen Kane*. Johnson's essay, while it treats *Kane* as the *chef-d'oeuvre,* surveys the whole of Welles's production in film and establishes brilliantly the distinctive qualities of Welles's subject matter, style and vision—those preoccupations, perspectives, and devices which constitute his signature. Together the interview and general essay provide a context for the more detailed material on *Kane* which follows.

The reviews were written under widely varying circumstances. O'Hara's prerelease notice helps to indicate the context of controversy into which the film was born (and why many newspapers and journals conspired by silence to make the birth a still one). Crowther's initial enthusiasm and "allegedly second thoughts" reveal what was to be an often-repeated dissatisfaction with the depiction of the character of Kane and a critical bias which demands that a film solve rather than pose problems. The two pieces also hint at a disbelief that the first film by a man as young as Welles could be truly "great." Ferguson's claim that it takes years and years to learn how to make a fine film is another version of this biographical nonargument, but at least he tries to relate it to estimates of the use of techniques and the editing process. The longer magazine reviews of Belfrage and Lean, while not without their own negative assessments of various elements, respond much more richly and positively to the theme and craftsmanship of the film —both visual and aural.

The heart of the volume consists of the essays which follow, and which variously treat the film's sociopolitical, historical, autobiographical, dramatic, technical, and poetic dimensions. It is in these essays that one begins to discover what Welles borrowed, stole, and adapted from his predecessors and what, uniquely, he did with these absorbed thematic and technical conventions. One begins to see, in short, what is special about *Citizen Kane* and why it has emerged as more than just another story of a money and power-corrupted man incapable of love and why it has achieved its reputation as the best film ever made in America.

Welles's statements that *Kane* "is never judged with the objectivity of an author" and that "the point of the picture is not so much the solution of the problem as its presentation" offered a crucial clue which has not been sufficiently followed even to this day. One could hardly hope to find more satisfactory—because succinct and lucid—accounts of the cinematographic and aural inventiveness that marks *Kane* than those provided by Gregg Toland and Bernard Herrmann.[1] One begins to sense from these creative participants the extraordinary care that was lavished on every detail of the film, to appreciate the remarkable quality of the (mostly) young and inventive production team and to grasp the extent to which Welles displayed in his first film the integrating field-generalship which he has spoken of as an essential talent of the successful director.

I was astonished to discover that Roy Fowler's pioneering little book on Welles was written when he was seventeen years old. From the selections reprinted here one learns about Welles's pre-Hollywood careers in radio and theatre, about the abortive attempts to film *Heart of Darkness* and *Smiler with a Knife*, about the prerelease duels with Hearst, and finally about the reception of the film. This important biographical and production background information is essentially accurate and is presented gracefully. The abundance of "amazings" and similarly enthusiastic adjectives in the critical discussion of the film may betray a youthful excess of zeal, but the analysis covers briefly all aspects of the film and holds its own without apology.

Sarris's retrospective essay deals very effectively with the relations among content ("themes"), the shape Welles gives that content (what Sarris calls its "structure") and the film's much-discussed techniques. Of particular interest is Sarris's emphasis on the distinctively American qualities in the career of Charles Foster Kane and his reminder of the highly charged political atmosphere into which the film was born— an atmosphere which desired—even needed—the film to be an anti-Fascist attack on Hearst.

Peter Cowie's book on Welles is still the best introduction in English to Welles's achievement in cinema, and his chapter on *Citizen Kane* is a model survey and analysis of a film—balanced, shrewd, and original. Without merely name and title-dropping, Cowie establishes the narrative and technical legacy Welles inherited from European and American directors and hints at the impact *Kane* has had on later generations of cinéastes. Arthur Knight's brief essay, with its focus on a few distinctive features of *Citizen Kane*, provides a nice coda and brings the sampling of criticism up to date.

The commentaries offer either brief estimates or material excerpted

---

[1] Additional reflections by Toland on his work on *Kane* may be found in "The Motion Picture Cameraman," *Theatre Arts Monthly* 25 (September 1941): 647-54. For a fully detailed analysis of this work and for further facts about Herrmann's complex musical score see the chapter on *Kane* in Charles Higham's *The Films of Orson Welles* (1970).

from longer works. Borges and Truffaut, despite their negative conclusions, offer some shrewd perceptions on the film's theme and technique. Bazin's book on Welles is excellent and this brief excerpt demonstrates nicely what is distinctively Wellesian in the direction. Higham's extended comparison and contrast of Hearst and Kane is by far the best of its kind; his summary estimate of the film tries to distribute praise and blame with even-handed justice. (With what success, each reader will have to decide.) Stephanick's short essay confirms the continuing impact of the film on students; the letter from the Production Code Office is worth including for what it suggests about the evolution of the screenplay and the extreme sociopolitical constraints that governed film production before the Second World War.

The concluding section of the book offers material which I believe will be useful for further study. Of course the availability of the complete screenplay will do much to enhance the careful study of the film. So will easier (and cheaper) access to the film—in television-usable film cartridges, for example.

What are the forms such study might take? I would argue that in general the study of film as art in America is no more advanced on its historical side than musicology was before World War I or, on its analytical side, than literary criticism before World War II. Whatever else it does, Charles Higham's recent book on Welles shows how much can and needs to be done with respect to assembling the facts about a film's conception, production, and release, about the incredibly complicated interdependence of contributors that is at once the bane and glory of film-making. On the critical side, even the excellent essays in this volume are simply not commensurate with their subject.

More specifically, there are a great many unanswered questions about *Citizen Kane,* a great many unexplored approaches to what I see as the wholeness, energy, and poetic richness of the film. The film has, as so few do, form. But whether that form derives more from the writing than from the directing is not clear. Nor is it yet clear—as between Welles and Herman J. Mankiewicz—who is responsible for what is in the screenplay. What was planned, what improvised in production? To what extent are the integration of form and content fortuitous, to what extent a tribute to Welles's integrating vision?

With respect to the "text" itself, many questions about larger elements of the film—narrative point of view and structure—have not been explored adequately. Keeping in mind that Welles wanted most of all to adapt *Heart of Darkness* as his first major film project, to what extent was Welles influenced by Conrad's preoccupation with multiple points of view, with the aesthetic and philosophical implications of the conclusion expressed by Conrad's friend and collaborator Ford Maddox Ford: ". . . we saw that Life did not narrate, but made impressions on our brains. We in turn, if we wished to produce on you an effect of life, must not narrate but render . . . impressions." [2] Thematic "borrowings" from Conrad—parallels between the characters of Mr. Kurtz and Charles Foster Kane, the ambiguity of truth, the radically divided nature of man—might also be investigated.

The analysis of the relation of parts to whole has only begun. How, for instance, do the mysterious, impressionistic, dreamlike qualities of the opening sequence relate to the factual, objective, realistic characteristics of the newsreel? What are the functions of the magical invocation and the documentary capsule? How do these relations and functions in turn relate to the symmetrically balancing closing sequences?

At the level of texture, *Kane* will also reward further scrutiny. Verbally and visually it is a work of which one can always ask: why this and why this and not something else? Why, for example, does the camera linger over the "K" at the entrance to Xanadu? Does this image become a motif? Does this motif have any relationship to theme or is it, like the monogram on Kane's shirt, merely decorative? What are some other motifs? Is the verbal pun of Kane's threat to send Gettys to Sing Sing intentional? Is there any calculated heightening of meaning in the visual-verbal pun which has Kane reassuring Susan "this is our home" precisely at the moment he steps into the God-sized fireplace at Xanadu? Why is it that Welles has Kane amuse Susan at their first meeting with a shadow-figure of a rooster (which she doesn't recognize)? Is the irony of the famous shock-cut to the shrieking cockatoo when she leaves him made more resonant by this parallel?

Though we know something of the immediate social and political background from which *Kane* emerged, its cinematic and thematic roots have not been fully traced to their sources of nourishment. Welles has acknowledged a technical and formal debt to Ford, but it is *Stagecoach* not *The Grapes of Wrath* that he pays tribute to; just how *Kane* fits into a late Depression context is far from clear. It is easy to discuss *Kane* as an example of the "lavish biography," and make allusions to "sociological and problem" films of the committed thirties, but the nature and extent of such relationships have not been demonstrated.

These are simply some of the more obvious questions one might ask. It is hoped that this volume will stimulate the reader to see the film again and again and to ask different and better ones. Like any important work of art, *Citizen Kane* both demands and is superior to repeated acts of attention.

[2] An interesting source or influence study might involve a careful study of Ford's *Joseph Conrad: A Personal Remembrance* (London, 1924). Such a study, of course, might further consider turn of the century developments in the art of fiction. It might also be interesting to consider the possible influence of F. Scott Fitzgerald, especially in view of the obvious parallels between Kane and Gatsby.

A Trip to Don Quixoteland: Conversations with Orson Welles
by JUAN COBOS, MIGUEL RUBIO, and J. A. PRUNEDA

Q: *What is astonishing in your work is this continual effort to bring solutions to the problems posed by directing. . . .*

WELLES: The cinema is still very young and it would be completely ridiculous to not succeed in finding new things for it. If only I could make more films! Do you know what happened with *The Trial?* Two weeks before our departure from Paris for Yugoslavia, we were told that there would be no possibility of having a single set built there because the producer had already made another film in Yugoslavia and hadn't paid his debts. That's why it was necessary to utilize that abandoned station. I had planned a completely different film.

Everything was invented at the last minute because physically my film had an entirely different conception. It was based on an absence of sets. And this gigantism I have been reproached for is, in part, due to the fact that the only set I possessed was that old abandoned station. An empty railroad station is immense! The production, as I had sketched it, comprised sets that gradually disappeared. The number of realistic elements were to become fewer and fewer and the public would become aware of it, to the point where the scene would be reduced to free space as if everything had dissolved.

Q: *The movement of the actors and the camera in relation to each other in your films is very beautiful.*

WELLES: That is a visual obsession. I believe, thinking about my

"*A Trip to Don Quixoteland: Conversations with Orson Welles*" by Juan Cobos, Miguel Rubio, and J. A. Pruneda, trans. Rose Kaplin, Cahiers du Cinéma (*English*), No. 5 (1966): 34–47. Reprinted by permission of Editions de l'Étoile and Grove Press, Inc.

films, that they are based not so much on pursuit as on a search. If we are looking for something, the labyrinth is the most favorable location for the search. I do not know why, but my films are all for the most part a physical search.

Q: *You reflect about your work a great deal.* . . .

WELLES: Never *a posteriori*. I think about each of my films when I am preparing for them. I do an enormous sketch when starting. What is marvelous about the cinema, what makes it superior to the theatre, is that it has many elements that may conquer us but may also enrich us, offer us a life impossible anywhere else. The cinema should always be the discovery of something. I believe that the cinema should be essentially poetic; that is why, during the shooting and not during the preparation, I try to plunge myself into a poetic development, which differs from narrative development and dramatic development. But, in reality, I am a man of ideas; yes, above all else—I am even more a man of ideas than a moralist, I suppose.

Q: *Do you believe it is possible to have a form of tragedy without melodrama?*

WELLES: Yes, but that is very difficult. For any *auteur* who comes out of the Anglo-Saxon tradition, it is very difficult. Shakespeare never arrived at it. It is possible, but up to the present no one has succeeded. In my cultural tradition, tragedy cannot escape from melodrama. We may always draw from tragic elements and perhaps even the grandeur of tragedy but melodrama is always inherent to the Anglo-Saxon cultural universe. There's no doubt about it.

Q: *Is it correct that your films never correspond to what you were thinking of doing before starting them? Because of producers, etc?*

WELLES: No, in reality, in what concerns me, creation, I must say that I am constantly changing. At the beginning, I have a basic notion of what the final aspect of the film will be, more or less. But each day, at every moment, one deviates or modifies because of the expression in an actress's eyes or the position of the sun. I am not in the habit of preparing a film and then setting myself to make it. I prepare a film but I have no intention of making *this* film. The preparation serves to liberate me, so that I may work in my fashion; thinking of bits of film and of the result they will give; and there are parts that deceive me because I haven't conceived them in a complete enough way. I do not know what word to use, because I am afraid of pompous words when I talk about making a film. The degree of concentration I utilize in a world that I create, whether this be for thirty seconds or for two hours, is very high; that is why, when I am shooting, I have a lot of trouble sleeping. This is not because I am preoccupied but because, for me, this world has so much reality that closing my eyes is not sufficient to make it disappear. It represents a terrible intensity of feeling. If I shoot in a royal location I sense and I see this site in so violent a way that, now, when I see these places again, they are similar to tombs, completely dead. There are spots in the world that are, to my eyes, cadavers; that is because I have already shot there—for me, they are completely finished. Jean Renoir said something that seems to be related to that: "We should remind people that a field of wheat painted by Van Gogh can arouse a stronger emotion than a field of wheat in nature." It is important to recall that art surpasses reality. Film becomes another reality. Apropos, I admire Renoir's work very much even though mine doesn't please him at all. We are good friends and, truthfully, one of the things I regret is that he doesn't like his films for the same reason I do. His films appear marvelous to me because what I admire most in an *auteur* is authentic sensitivity. I attach no importance to whether or not a film is a technical SUCCESS: moreover, films that lack this kind of sensitivity may not be judged on the same level with technical or aesthetic knowingness. But the cinema, the true cinema, is a poetic expression and Renoir is one of the rare poets. Like Ford, it is in his style. Ford is a poet. A comedian. Not for women, of course, but for men.

Q: *Apart from Ford and Renoir, who are the* cineástes *you admire?*

WELLES: Always the same ones; I believe that on this point I am not very original. The one who pleases me most of all is Griffith. I think he is the best director in the history of the cinema. The best, much better than Eisenstein. And, for all that, I admire Eisenstein very much. . . .

Q: *In your films, one has the sensation that real space is never respected: it seems not to interest you.* . . .

WELLES: The fact that I make no use of it doesn't in the least signify that it doesn't please me. In other terms, there are many elements of the cinematographic language that I do not utilize, but that is not because I have something against them. It seems to me that the field of action in which I have my experiences is one that is least known, and my duty is to explore it. But that does not mean to say that it is, for me, the best and only—or that I deviate from a normal conception of space, in relation to the camera. I believe that the artist should explore his means of expression.

In reality, the cinema, with the exception of a few little tricks that don't go very far, has not advanced for more than thirty years. The only changes are with respect to the subject of films. I see that there are directors, full of future, sensitive, who explore new themes, but I see no one who attacks form, the manner of saying things. That seems to interest no one. They resemble each other very much in terms of style.

Q: *You must work very quickly. In twenty-five years of cinema, you have made ten films, you have acted in thirty, you have made a series* of very long programs for television, you have acted and directed in the theatre, you have done narrations for other films and, in addition, you have written thirty scenarios. Each of them must have taken you more than six months.

WELLES: Several of them even longer. There are those that took me two years but that is because I set them aside from time to time in order to do something else and picked them up again afterwards. But it is also true that I write very rapidly.

Q: *You write them completely, with dialogue?*

WELLES: I always begin with the dialogue. And I do not understand how one dares to write action before dialogue. It's a very strange conception. I know that in theory the word is secondary in cinema but the secret of my work is that everything is based on the word. I do not make silent films. I must begin with what the characters say. I must know what they say before seeing them do what they do.

Q: *However, in your films the visual part is essential.*

WELLES: Yes, but I couldn't arrive at it without the solidity of the word taken as a basis for constructing the images. What happens is that when the visual components are shot the words are obscured. The most classical example is *Lady from Shanghai*. The scene in the aquarium was so gripping visually that no one heard what was being said. And what was said was, for all that, the marrow of the film. The subject was so tedious that I said to myself, "This calls for something beautiful to look at." Assuredly, the scene was very beautiful. The first ten minutes of the film did not please me at all. When I think of them I have the impression it wasn't me that made them. They resemble any Hollywood film. . . .

Q: *How do you work with actors?*

WELLES: I give them a great deal of freedom and, at the same time, the feeling of precision. It's a strange combination. In other words, physically, and in the way they develop, I demand the precision of ballet. But their way of acting comes directly from their own ideas as much as from mine. When the camera begins to roll, I do not improvise visually. In this realm, everything is prepared. But I work very freely with the actors. I try to make their life pleasant.

Q: *Your cinema is essentially dynamic. . . .*

WELLES: I believe that the cinema should be dynamic although I suppose any artist will defend his own style. For me, the cinema is a slice of life in movement that is projected on a screen; it is not a frame. I do not believe in the cinema unless there is movement on the screen. This is why I am not in agreement with certain directors, whom, however, I admire, who content themselves with a static cinema. For me, these are dead images. I hear the noise of the projector behind me, and when I see these long, long walks along streets, I am always waiting to hear the director's voice saying, "Cut!"

The only director who does not move either his camera or his actors very much, and in whom I believe, is John Ford. He succeeds in making me believe in his films even though there is little movement in them. But with the others I always have the impression that they are desperately trying to make Art. However, they should be making drama and drama should be full of life. The cinema, for me, is essentially a dramatic medium, not a literary one.

Q: *That is why your mise-en-scène is lively: it is the meeting of two movements, that of the actors and that of the camera. Out of this flows an anguish that reflects modern life very well.* . . .

WELLES: I believe that that corresponds to my vision of the world; it reflects that sort of vertigo, uncertainty, lack of stability, that *mélange* of movement and tension that is our universe. And the cinema should express that. Since cinema has the pretension of being an art, it should be, above all, film, and not the sequel to another, more literary, medium of expression.

Q: *Herman G. Weinberg said, while speaking of* Mr. Arkadin, *"In Orson Welles's films, the spectator may not sit back in his seat and relax, on the contrary he must meet the film at least halfway in order to decipher what is happening, practically every second; if not, everything is lost."*

WELLES: All my films are like that. There are certain *cineástes*, excellent ones, who present everything so explicitly, so clearly, that in spite of the great visual power contained in their films one follows them effortlessly—I refer only to the narrative thread. I am fully aware that, in my films, I demand a very specific interest on the part of the public. Without that attention, it is lost.

Q: *Lady from Shanghai is a story that, filmed by another director, would more likely have been based on sexual questions.* . . .

WELLES: You mean that another director would have made it more obvious. I do not like to show sex on the screen crudely. Not because of morality or puritanism; my objection is of a purely aesthetic order. In my opinion, there are two things that can absolutely not be carried to the screen: the realistic presentation of the sexual act and praying to God. I never believe an actor or actress who pretends to be completely involved in the sexual act if it is too literal, just as I can never believe an actor who wants to make me believe he is praying. These are two things that, for me, immediately evoke the presence of a projector and a white screen, the existence of a series of technicians and a director who is saying, "Good. Cut." And I imagine them in the process of preparing for the next shot. As for those who adopt a mystical stance and look fervently at the spotlights. . . .

For all that, my illusion almost never ends when I see a film. While filming, I think of someone like myself: I utilize all of my knowledge in order to force this person to want to see the film with the greatest interest, I want him to believe what is there on the screen; this means that one should create a real world there. I place my dramatic vision of a character in the world . . . if not, the film is something dead. What there is on the screen is nothing but shadows. Something even more dead than words.

Q: *Do you like comedy?*

WELLES: I have written at least five scenarios for comedy and in the theatre I have done more comedies than dramas. Comedy fills me with enthusiasm but I have never succeeded in getting a film producer to let me make one. One of the best things I did for television was a program in the genre of comedy. For example, I like Hawks's comedies very much. I even wrote about twenty-five minutes of one of them. It was called, *I Was a Male War Bride*. The scenarist fell ill and I wrote almost a third of the film. . . .

Q: *There is a kinship between your work and the works of certain authors of the modern theatre, like Beckett, Ionesco, and others . . . what is called the theatre of the absurd.*

WELLES: Perhaps, but I would eliminate Ionesco because I do not admire him. When I directed *Rhinoceros* in London, with Laurence Olivier in the principal role, as we repeated the work from day to day it pleased me less. I believe that there is nothing inside it. Nothing at all. This kind of theatre comes out of all types of expression, all types of art of a certain epoch, is thus forged by the same world as my films. The things this theatre is composed of are the same composed in my films, without this theatre's being in my cinema or without my cinema's being in this theatre. It is a trait of our times. There is where the coincidence comes from.

Q: *There are two types of artists: for example, Velasquez and Goya; one disappears from the picture, the other is present in it; on the other hand you have Van Gogh and Cezanne. . . .*

WELLES: I see what you mean. It's very clear.

Q: *It seems to me that you are on the Goya side.*

WELLES: Doubtless. But I very much prefer Velasquez. There's no comparison between one and the other, as far as being artists is concerned. As I prefer Cezanne to Van Gogh.

Q: *And between Tolstoy and Dostoievsky?*

WELLES: I prefer Tolstoy.

Q: *But as an artist. . . .*

WELLES: Yes, as an artist. But I deny that, for I do not correspond to my tastes. I know what I'm doing and when I recognize it in other works my interest is diminished. The things that resemble me the least are the things that interest me the most. For me Velasquez is the Shakespeare of painters and, for all that, he has nothing in common with my way of working.

Q: *What do you think of what is called modern cinema?*

WELLES: I like certain young French cineástes, much more than the Italians.

Q: *Did you like* L'Année dernière à Marienbad?

WELLES: No. I know that this film pleased you; not me. I held on up to the fourth reel and after that I left at a run. It reminded me too much of *Vogue* magazine.

Q: *How do you see the development of the cinema?*

WELLES: I don't see it. I rarely go to the movies. There are two kinds of writers, the writer who reads everything of interest that is published, exchanges letters with other writers, and others who absolutely do not read their contemporaries. I am among the latter. I go to the movies very rarely and this is not because I don't like them, it is because they give me no enjoyment at all. I do not think I am very intelligent about films. There are works that I know to be good but which I cannot stand.

Q: *It was said that you were going to make* Crime and Punishment; *what became of this project?*

WELLES: Someone wanted me to do it. I thought about it, but I like the book too much. In the end, I decided that I could do nothing and the idea of being content to illustrate it did not please me at all. I don't mean to say by that that the subject was beneath me, what I mean is that I could bring nothing to it. I could only give it actors and images and, when I can only do that, the cinema does not interest me. I believe you must say something new about a book, otherwise it is better not to touch it.

Aside from that, I consider it to be a very difficult work, because, in my opinion, it is not completely comprehensible outside of its own time and country. The psychology of this man and this constable are so Russian, so nineteenth-century Russian, that one could never find them elsewhere; I believe that the public would not be able to follow it all the way.

Q: *There is, in Dostoievsky, an analysis of justice, of the world, that is very close to yours.*

WELLES: Perhaps too close. My contribution would most likely be limited. The only thing I could do is to direct. I like to make films in which I can express myself as *auteur* rather than as interpreter. I do not share Kafka's point of view in *The Trial.* I believe that he is a good writer, but Kafka is not the extraordinary genius that people today see him as. That is why I was not concerned about excessive fidelity and could make a film by Welles. If I could make four films a year, I would surely do *Crime and Punishment*. But as it costs me a great deal to convince producers I try to choose what I film very carefully.

Q: *With you, one seems to find, at the same time, the Brechtian tendency and the Stanislavski tendency.*

WELLES: All I can say is that I did my apprenticeship in Stanislavski's orbit; I worked with his actors and found them very easy to direct. I do not allude to "Method" actors; that's something else altogether. But Stanislavski was marvelous. As for Brecht, he was a great friend to me. We worked together on *Galileo Galilei*. In reality he wrote it for me. Not for me to act in, but in order for me to direct it.

Q: *How was Brecht?*

WELLES: Terribly nice. He had an extraordinary brain. One could see very well that he had been educated by the Jesuits. He had the type of disciplined brain characterized by Jesuit education. Instinctively, he was more of an anarchist than a Marxist, but he believed himself a perfect Marxist. When I said to him one day, while we were talking about *Galileo*, that he had written a perfectly anticommunist work, he became nearly violent. I answered him, "But this Church you describe has to be Stalin and not the Pope, at this time. You have made something resolutely anti-Soviet!"

Q: *What relationship do you see between your work as a film director and as a theatre director?*

WELLES: My relationships with these two *milieux* are very different. I believe that they are not in intimate rapport, one with the other. Perhaps in me, as a man, that relationship exists, but technical solutions are so different for each of them that, in my spirit, I establish absolutely no relationship between these two mediums.

In the theatre, I do not belong to what has succeeded in becoming the Brechtian idea of theatre; that particularly withdrawn form has never been appropriate to my character. But I have always made a terrible effort to recall to the public, at each instant, that it is in a theatre. I have never tried to bring it into the scene, I have rather tried to bring the scene to it. And that is the opposite of the cinema.

Q: *Perhaps there is a relationship in the way the actors are handled.*

WELLES: In the theatre there are 1,500 cameras rolling at the same time—in the cinema there is only one. That changes the whole aesthetic for the director.

Q: *Did Huston's* Moby Dick, *on which you worked, please you?*

WELLES: The novel pleases me very much, but it doesn't please me as a novel so much as a drama. There are two very different things in the novel: that sort of pseudo-biblical element that is not very good, and also that curious nineteenth-century American element, of the apocalyptical genre, that can be rendered very well in the cinema.

Q: *In the scene you acted in the film—did you make any suggestions as to the way of handling it?*

WELLES: All we did was discuss the way in which it would be shot. You know that my discourse is very long. It goes on throughout a full reel, and we never repeated it. I arrived on the set already made-up and dressed. I got up on the platform and we shot it in one take. We did it using only one camera angle. And that is one of Huston's merits, because another director would have said, "Let's do it from another angle and see what we get." He said, "Good," and my role in the film ended right there! . . .

Q: *There is talk from time to time of your first sojourn in Spain, before the Civil War.*

WELLES: When I arrived in Spain, for the first time, I was seventeen years old and had already worked in Ireland as an actor. I only stayed in the south, in Andalusia. In Seville, I lived in the Triana section. I was writing detective stories: I spent only two days a week on this and it brought in three hundred dollars. With this money I was a *grand seigneur* in Seville. There were so many people thrilled by the *corrida* and I caught the virus myself. I paid the novice fee at several *corridas* and thus was able to *debut*—on the posters I was called "The American." My greatest thrill was being able to practice the *metier* of *torero* three or four times without having to pay. I came to the realization that I was not good as a *torero* and decided to apply myself to writing. At that time I hardly thought of the theatre and still less of the cinema.

Q: *You said one day that you have had a great deal of difficulty finding the money to make your films, that you have spent more time struggling to get this money than working as an artist. How is this battle at this time?*

WELLES: More bitter than ever. Worse than ever. Very difficult. I have already said that I do not work enough. I am frustrated, do you understand? And I believe that my work shows that I do not do enough filming. My cinema is perhaps too explosive, because I wait too long before I speak. It's terrible. I have bought little cameras in order to make a film if I can find the money. I will shoot it in 16 mm. The cinema is a *metier* . . . nothing can compare to the cinema. The cinema belongs to our times. It is "the thing" to do. During the shooting of *The Trial,* I spent marvelous days. It was an amusement, happiness. You cannot imagine what I felt.

When I make a film or at the time of my theatrical premieres, the critics habitually say, "This work is not as good as the one of three years ago." And if I look for the criticism of that one, three years back, I find an unfavorable review that says that that isn't as good as what I did three years earlier. And so it goes. I admit that experiences can be false but I believe that it is also false to want to be fashionable. If one is fashionable for the greatest part of one's career, one will produce second-class work. Perhaps by chance one will arrive at being a success but this means that one is a follower and not an innovator. An artist should lead, blaze trails.

What is serious is that in countries where English is spoken, the role played by criticism concerning serious works of cinema is very important. Given the fact that one cannot make films in competition with Doris Day, what is said by reviews such as *Sight and Sound* is the only reference.

Things are going particularly badly in my own country. *Touch of Evil* never had a first-run, never had the usual presentation to the press, and was not the object of any critical writing in either the weeklies, the reviews, or the daily papers. It was considered to be too bad. When the representative from Universal wanted to exhibit it at the Brussels Fair in 1958, he was told that it wasn't a good enough film for a festival. He answered that, in any case, it must be put on the program. It went unnoticed and was sent back. The film took the *grand prix*, but it was no less sent back.

Q: *Do you consider yourself a moralist?*

WELLES: Yes, but against morality. Most of the time that may appear paradoxical, but the things I love in painting, in music, in literature, represent only my penchant for what is my opposite. And moralists bore me very much. However, I'm afraid I am one of them!

Q: *In what concerns you, it is not so much a question of a moralist's attitude but rather an ethic that you adopt in the face of the world.*

WELLES: My two Shakespearean films are made from an ethical point of view. I believe I have never made a film without having a solid ethical point of view about its story. Morally speaking, there is no ambiguity in what I do.

Q: *But an ambiguous point of view is necessary. These days, the world is made that way.*

WELLES: But that is the way the world appears to us. It is not a true ambiguity: it's like a larger screen. A kind of a moral cinemascope. I believe it is necessary to give all the characters their best arguments, in order that they may defend themselves, including those I disagree with. To them as well, I give the best defensive arguments I can imagine. I offer them the same possibility for expression as I would a sympathetic character.

That's what gives this impression of ambiguity: my being chivalrous to people whose behavior I do not approve of. The characters are ambiguous but the significance of the work is not. I do not want to resemble the majority of Americans, who are demagogs and rhetoricians. This is one of America's great weaknesses, and rhetoric is one of the greatest weaknesses of American artists; above all, those of my generation. Miller, for example, is terribly rhetorical.

Q: *What is the problem in America?*

WELLES: If I speak to you of the things that are wrong it won't be the obvious ones; those are similar to what is wrong in France, in Italy, or in Spain; we know them all. In American art the problem, or better, one of the problems, is the betrayal of the Left by the Left, selfbetrayal. In one sense, by stupidity, by orthodoxy, and because of slogans; in another, by simple betrayal. We are very few in our generation who have not betrayed our position, who have not given other people's names. . . .

That is terrible. It can never be undone. I don't know how one starts over after a similar betrayal that, however, differs enormously from this, for example: a Frenchman who collaborated with the gestapo in order to save his wife's life—that is another genre of collaboration. What is so bad about the American Left is that it betrayed in order to save its swimming pools. There was no American Right in my generation. Intellectually it didn't exist. There were only Leftists and they mutually betrayed each other. The Left was not destroyed by McCarthy: it demolished itself, ceding to a new generation of Nihilists. That's what happened.

You can't call it "Fascism." I believe that the term "Fascism" should only be utilized in order to define a quite precise political attitude. It would be necessary to find a new word in order to define what is happening in America. Fascism must be born out of chaos. And America is not, as I know it, in chaos. The social structure is not in a state of dissolution. No, it doesn't correspond at all to the true definition of Fascism. I believe it is two simple, obvious things: the technological society is not accustomed to living with its own tools. That's what counts. We speak of them, we use them but we don't know how to live with them. The other thing is the prestige of the people responsible for the technological society. In this society the men who direct and the savants who represent technique do not leave room for the artist who favors the human being. In reality, they utilize him only for decoration.

Hemingway says, in *The Green Hills of Africa,* that America is a country of adventure and, if the adventure disappears there, any American who possesses this primitive spirit must go elsewhere to seek adventure: Africa, Europe, etc. . . . It is an intensely romantic point of view. There is some truth in it, but if it is so intensely romantic it is because there is still an enormous quantity of adventure in America. In the cinema, you cannot imagine all that one may do in it. All I need is a job in cinema, is for someone to give me a camera. There is nothing dishonorable about working in America. The country is full of possibilities for expressing what is happening all over the world. What really exists is an enormous compromise. The ideal American type is perfectly expressed by the Protestant, individualist, anticonformist, and this is the type that is in the process of disappearing. In reality, a very few of him remain. . . .

Q: *As an artist and as a member of a certain generation, do you feel isolated?*

WELLES: I have always felt isolated. I believe that any good artist feels isolated. And I must think that I am a good artist, for otherwise I would not be able to work and I beg your pardon for taking the liberty of believing this; if someone wants to direct a film, he must think that he is good. A good artist should be isolated. If he isn't isolated, something is wrong.

Q: *These days, it would be impossible to present the Mercury Theatre.*

WELLES: Completely impossible for financial reasons. The Mercury Theatre was possible only because I was earning three thousand dollars a week on the radio and spending two thousand to sustain the theatre. At that time, it was still cheap to sustain a theatre. Plus I had formidable actors. And what was most exciting about this Mercury Theatre was that it was a theatre on Broadway, not "off." Today, one might have a theatre off-Broadway, but that's another thing.

What characterized the Mercury Theatre was that it was next door to another where they were doing a musical comedy, near a commercial theatre, it was in the theatre center. Part of the neighboring bill of fare was the Group Theatre which was the official theatre of the Left: we were in contact without having an official relationship; we were of the same generation, although not on the same path. The whole thing gave the New York of that time an extraordinary vitality. The quality of actors and that of spectators is no longer what it was in those marvelous years. The best theatre should be in the center of everything.

Q: *Does that explain your permanent battle to remain in the milieu of the cinema and not outside of the industry?*

WELLES: I may be rejected, but as for me, I always want to be right in the center. If I am isolated, it is because I am obliged to be, for such is not my intention. I am always aiming for the center. I fail, but that is what I try to attain.

Q: *Are you thinking of returning to Hollywood?*

WELLES: Not at the moment. But who knows what may change at the next instant? . . . I am dying to work there because of the technicians, who are marvelous. They truly represent a director's dream.

Q: *A certain anti-Fascist attitude can be found in your films.* . . .

WELLES: There is more than one French intellectual who believes that I am a Fascist . . . it's idiotic, but that's what they write. What happens with these French intellectuals is that they take my physical aspect as an actor for my idea as an *auteur*. As an actor I always play a certain type of role: Kings, great men, etc. This is not because I think them to be the only persons in the world who are worth the trouble. My physical aspect does not permit me to play other roles. No one would believe a defenseless, humble person played by me. But they take this to be a projection of my own personality. I hope that the great majority at least considers it obvious that I am anti-Fascist. . . .

True Fascism is always confused with Futurism's early fascistic mystique. By this I make allusion to the first generation of Italian Fascism, which was a way of speaking that disappeared as soon as the true Fascism imposed itself, because it was an idiotic romanticism, like that of d'Annunzio and others. That is what disappeared. And that is what the French critics are talking about.

True Fascism is gangsterism of the low-born middle class, lamentably organized by . . . good, we all know what Fascism is. It is very clear. It is amusing to see how the Russians have been mistaken about the subject of *Touch of Evil*. They have attacked it pitilessly, as if it were a question of the veritable decadence of Western civilization. They were not content to attack what I showed: they attacked me too.

I believe that the Russians didn't understand the words, or some other thing. What is disastrous, in Russia, is that they are fully in the middle ages, the middle ages in its most rigid aspect. No one thinks for himself. It is very sad. This orthodoxy has something terrible about it. They live only by slogans they have inherited. No one any longer knows what these slogans signify. . . .

Q: *You are often accused of being egocentric. When you appear as an actor in your films, it is said that the camera is, above all, in the service of your personal exhibition. . . . For example, in* Touch of Evil *the shooting angle moves from a general shot to a close-up in order to catch your first appearance on getting out of the car.*

WELLES: Yes, but that is the story, the subject. I wouldn't act a role if it was not felt as dominating the whole story. I do not think it is just [,however,] to say that I utilize the camera to my profit and not to the profit of the other actors. It's not true. Although they will say it even more about *Falstaff*: but it is precisely because in the film I am playing Falstaff, not Hotspur.

At this time I think and rethink, above all, of the world in which the story unfolds, of the appearance of the film. The number of sets I will be able to build will be so restrained that the film will have to be resolutely anti-Baroque. It will have to have numerous rather formal general shots, like what one may see at eye level, wall frescoes. It is a big problem creating a world in period costumes. In this genre, it is diffi-

Throughout the entire European cinema industry, to a greater or lesser degree, one feels that there is a great barrier posed by educational differences. In all European countries one is called "Doctor," "Professor," etc., if one has gone to a university; the great advantage in America is that there, at times, you find directors who are less learned than the man who pushes the camera. There is no "professor." Classes do not exist in the American cinema world. The pleasure one experiences working with an American crew is something that has no equivalent on earth. But you pay a price for that. There are the producers, and that group is as bad as the technicians are good. . . .

Q: *What do you think of the American cinema, as seen from Europe?*

WELLES: I am surprised by the tendency of the serious critics to find elements of value only among the American directors of action films, while they find none in the American directors of historical films. Lubitsch, for example, is a giant. But he doesn't correspond to the taste of cinema aesthetes. Why? I know nothing about it. Besides, it doesn't interest me. But Lubitsch's talent and originality are stupefying.

Q: *And Von Sternberg?*

WELLES: Admirable! He is the greatest exotic director of all time and one of the great lights.

Q: *Let's talk about other directors. What do you think of Arthur Penn? Have you seen* The Left-Handed Gun?

WELLES: I saw it first on television and then as cinema. It was better on television, more brutal, and beyond that I believe that at that time Penn had more experience directing for television and so handled it better, but for cinema this experience went against him. I believe him to be a good theatre director, an admirable director of actresses—a very rare thing: very few *cineastes* possess that quality.

I have seen nothing by the most recent generation, except for a sampling of the avante-garde. Among those whom I would call "younger generation" Kubrick appears to me to be a giant.

Q: *But, for example,* The Killing *was more or less a copy of* The Asphalt Jungle?

WELLES: Yes, but *The Killing* was better. The problem of imitation leaves me indifferent, above all if the imitator succeeds in surpassing the model. For me, Kubrick is a better director than Huston. I haven't seen *Lolita* but I believe that Kubrick can do everything. He is a great director who has not yet made his great film. What I see in him is a talent not possessed by the great directors of the generation immediately preceding his, I mean Ray, Aldrich, etc. Perhaps this is because his temperament comes closer to mine.

Q: *And those of the older generation? Wyler, for example? and Hitchcock?*

WELLES: Hitchcock is an extraordinary director; William Wyler a brilliant producer.

Q: *How do you make this distinction between two men who are both called directors?*

WELLES: A producer doesn't make anything. He chooses the story, works on it with the scenarist, has a say in the distribution, and, in the old sense of the term American producer, even decides on the camera angles, what sequences will be used. What is more, he defines the final form of the film. In reality, he is a sort of director's boss.

Wyler is this man. Only he's his own boss. His work, however, is better as boss than as director, given the fact that in that role he spends his clearest moments waiting, with the camera, for something to happen. He says nothing. He waits, as the producer waits in his office. He looks at twenty impeccable shots, seeking the one that has something, and usually he knows how to choose the best one. As a director he is good but as a producer he is extraordinary.

Q: *According to you, the role of director consists in making something happen?*

WELLES: I do not like to set up very strict rules, but in the Hollywood system, the director has one job. In other systems he has another job. I am against absolute rules because even in the case of America we find marvelous films achieved under the absolute tyranny of the production system. There are even films much respected by film societies that weren't made by directors but by producers and scenarists. . . . Under the American system, no one is capable of saying whether a film was or was not directed by a director.

Q: *In an interview, John Houseman said that you got all of the credit for* Citizen Kane *and that this was unfair because it should have gone to Herman J. Mankiewicz, who wrote the scenario.*

WELLES: He wrote several important scenes. (Houseman is an old enemy of mine.) I was very lucky to work with Mankiewicz: everything concerning Rosebud belongs to him. As for me, sincerely, he doesn't please me very much; he functions, it is true, but I have never had complete confidence in him. He serves as a hyphen between all the elements. I had, in return, the good fortune to have Gregg Toland, who is the best director of photography that ever existed, and I also had the luck to hit upon actors who had never worked in films before; not a single one of them had ever found himself in front of a camera until then. They all came from my theatre. I could never have made *Citizen Kane* with actors who were old hands at cinema, because they would have said right off, "Just what do you think we're doing?" My being a newcomer would have put them on guard and, with the same blow, would have made a mess of the film. It was possible because I had my own family, so to speak.

Q: *How did you arrive at* Citizen Kane's *cinematic innovations?*

WELLES: I owe it to my ignorance. If this word seems inadequate to you, replace it with innocence. I said to myself: this is what the camera should be really capable of doing, in a normal fashion. When we were on the point of shooting the first sequence, I said, "Let's do that!" Gregg Toland answered that it was impossible. I came back with, "We can always try; we'll soon see. Why not?" We had to have special lenses made because at that time there weren't any like those that exist today.

Q: *During the shooting, did you have the sensation of making such an important film?*

WELLES: I never doubted it for a single instant.

Orson Welles: Of Time and Loss
by WILLIAM JOHNSON

Judged by first—even second or third—impressions, Welles's films are a triumph of show over substance. His most memorable images seem like elephantine labors to bring forth mouse-size ideas.

His films bulge with preposterously vast spaces: the echoing halls of Kane's Xanadu; the rambling castles of Macbeth, Othello, and Arkadin; the vertiginous offices of *The Trial*; the cathedral-like palace and tavern of *Falstaff*.

His camera moves with a swagger, craning down through the skylight of El Rancho in *Kane* and up over the bomb-carrying car in *Touch of Evil*. When the camera is still, the composition may cry out for attention with anything from multiple reflections (the hall of mirrors in *Lady from Shanghai*) to a flurry of silhouettes (the battle in *Falstaff*).

The action often runs along the edge of violence, and sometimes topples over with a spectacular splash: Kane destroying Susan's room after she leaves him; Mike's brawl in the judge's office in *Lady from Shanghai*; Macbeth overturning the huge banquet table after Banquo's ghost appears; Vargas running amuck in the bar in *Touch of Evil*. At other times Welles expresses his love of spectacle in a show-within-a-show: the dancing girls at Kane's newspaper party and the opera in which Susan stars; the magician's act in *Journey into Fear*;[1] the Chinese theater in *Lady from Shanghai;* the flea circus in *Arkadin;* the slide show that begins and ends *The Trial*.

What makes all these Barnum qualities really seem to stick on Welles the director is the style and appearance of Welles the actor.

"Orson Welles: Of Time and Loss" by William Johnson. From Film Quarterly *21 (1967): 13–24. Copyright © 1967 by the Regents of the University of California. Reprinted by permission of the Regents.*

[1] Welles's hand in *Journey*, officially directed by Norman Foster, is uncertain, and I have avoided citing any further examples from this film.

With the sole exception of *Magnificent Ambersons,* the bravura manner of Welles's films centers around characters that he himself plays. It is Welles whose voice booms across the cavernous drawing room of Xanadu, it is Welles who overturns the banquet table at Glamis castle, it is Welles who conducts the slide show in *The Trial.* And the Barnum image is reinforced by his roles in other people's films, from the tongue-in-cheek sophistries of Harry Lime in *The Third Man* to the flamboyant magic of Le Chiffre in *Casino Royale.*

Of course, showmanship can be sublime, and even the harshest critics of Welles's films have some kind words for *Citizen Kane.* Judged simply by its style, the film must be accounted an impressive achievement for any director, let alone a 25-year-old newcomer to the movie medium. Many of the stylistic effects that Welles used with such apparent ease in *Kane* have become common screen currency only during the last ten years—wide-angle perspective, unusually long takes, abrupt cuts, intricate leaps in time, terse vignettes, heightened natural sound, and so on. Though precedents can be found for each of these devices, Welles was the first director to develop them into a full-blown style. With the exception of some typical forties process shots, the whole of *Kane* looks and sounds almost as modern today as it did in 1941—a good deal more modern, in fact, than many films of 1967.

Moreover, Welles's protean style clearly reflects the character of Kane—himself a kind of Barnum who conceals his private self behind a dazzling set of public images. It's possible for a critic to see no deeper into *Kane* than this and still give the film high marks for matching style and content.

Judged by these standards, Welles's other films are inferior. Neither their stylistic inventiveness nor their matching of style and content stands out so obviously as *Kane*'s. After a brilliant start, Welles's directing career seems to decline into potboilers (*Stranger, Lady from Shanghai, Touch of Evil*), distortions of literary originals (the Shakespeare films and *Trial*) and a rehash of *Kane*—*Arkadin*—which demonstrates only too clearly the coarsening of his showmanship.

The foregoing view of Welles is, I believe, utterly wrong, and yet it has plausibility because it rests on a few points of truth. *Arkadin,* for example, *is* an inferior rehash of *Kane,* with grotesques instead of characters and with episodes loosely strung together instead of interlocking. *Macbeth,* with or without due allowance for the conditions under which it was made, *is* often ludicrous. There are other examples which I will come to later.

But it's difficult to maintain a balanced view of Welles's strengths and weaknesses. While his detractors see little but empty showiness, anyone who likes most of his work runs the risk of slipping to the opposite extreme. With a filmmaker as vigorous and idiosyncratic as Welles, it's temptingly easy to find some justification for nearly everything he does. *Arkadin* is based on an exciting and fruitful idea; some of the sequences in the film are excellent; many others are exciting or fascinating—and so I could go on, justifying the film piece by piece to the conclusion that it is all good. But here I'd be falling into the same trap as those who deny the originality of *Kane* because (for example) Renoir had previously used deep focus. It's the total effect that counts, and just as the total effect of Welles's deep focus is quite different from Renoir's, and much more far-reaching, so the total effect of *Arkadin* falls far short of its piecemeal felicities.

Similarly, Welles's films *are* showy, but this is only one side of them. The other, quieter side gives a far better clue to what his films are all about.

One of the finest scenes in *Kane* features no craning or dollying, no dramatic chiaroscuro, no optical distortions, no unusual sound effects, no jump cuts or, for that matter, cuts of any kind whatsoever. The reporter visits Kane's former lawyer, Bernstein, to see if he can explain "Rosebud." Bernstein suggests that it may have referred to some very fleeting experience in Kane's past, and cites as an example his own memory of a girl dressed in white whom he glimpsed forty years earlier. "I only saw her for a second," says Bernstein, "and she didn't see me at all, but I bet a month hasn't gone by that I haven't thought about her." Throughout the scene the camera remains absolutely still: all one sees is the back of the reporter's head, Bernstein at his desk, and rain falling outside the window. This unexpected plumbing of the depths of the cheery Bernstein is made all the more moving by the sudden stillness with which Welles films it.

One of Welles's films—*Magnificent Ambersons*—is nearly all stillness, or only the most leisurely of movements. Its tempo is set by the horse and buggy typical of the age that is ending when the film's action takes place. There is indeed an extremely long, gentle dolly shot that follows George and Lucy as they ride a buggy together through the town. But the basic tempo extends even to Gene Morgan (Joseph Cotten), the man who is hastening the death of the horse-and-buggy age by designing automobiles: he walks with an easy-going gait, and he talks with measured reasonableness even under verbal attack from the arrogant George.

The elegiac mood of *Ambersons* sets it apart from the rest of Welles's films, but its theme recurs in all of them, sometimes burrowing deep beneath the surface, sometimes coming out into the open as in the Bernstein reminiscence. This theme can be summed up as loss of innocence.

Bernstein's regret for a bright moment of his youth is a minor variation of the theme. It is Kane himself who provides the first and most sustained example of lost innocence—though it is one that may easily be misunderstood. Because Freudian symbolism was just creeping into Hollywood films when *Kane* appeared, the sled named Rosebud was widely seized upon as a psychoanalytic key to Kane's character. It is a simpler and more lyrical symbol—of Kane's childhood innocence that cannot be recovered.

Welles does not, of course, thrust a symbol at us and leave it at that. He has designed the whole film so as to bring Kane's predicament to life before our eyes; and he does this largely by giving an almost tangible presence to the passing of time. This might be called a 3-D film, with time instead of spatial depth as the salient third dimension. Nearly everything in the film contributes to this effect: the juxtaposition of scenes showing the different ages not only of Kane but also of those who know him, notably Jed Leland alternating between handsome youth and garrulous senility, Susan between wispy naïveté and sufficient toughness to leave Kane; the use of a different quality of image and sound in the newsreel of Kane's life, adding distance to the events featured in it and, by contrast, adding immediacy to the events filmed straight; and even such normally gimmicky devices as the dissolves from a still photograph to its subject in motion. Above all it is the structure of the film that brings Welles's theme to life. Two strands are intertwined throughout. In the film's present tense, there is the reporter's vain search for the meaning of Rosebud, which mirrors the aged Kane's own yearning for his lost innocence. Concurrently, the flashbacks into Kane's past follow him step by step as he loses that innocence. These alternating images of past and present fuse together stereoscopically into a powerful, poignant vision of Kane's loss.

Welles's other films present variations of this basic theme. Whereas *Kane* states it comprehensively, spanning almost a lifetime of change, several of the other films focus on particular stages: on the initial innocence of Mike in *Lady from Shanghai* and of Joseph K in *The Trial*; on the moment of loss for Macbeth and Othello; on a time long after the loss for Arkadin and for Hank Quinlan in *Touch of Evil*. In the other three films the theme is not tied so closely to a single character: in *The Stranger*, Nazi-in-hiding Franz Kindler threatens the innocent coziness of a New England village; in *Falstaff*, as in *Ambersons*, the loss of innocence lies in the transition between two historical ages.

Far from clashing with this lyrical theme, Welles's bravura qualities enrich it. Kane's onslaught on Susan's room comes to a halt when he sees the snow-scene paperweight: the sudden stillness, the whiteness of the paperweight as he cradles it in his hand, his whisper of "Rosebud" are all the more moving because of the lengthy destruction that went before. Similarly, in *Touch of Evil*—the most agitated of all Welles's films—the calm of Tanya's place draws a charge of lyrical power from the surrounding frenzy. The odd parlor, where a TV set is perched on top of a player piano, is like a time machine that whisks Quinlan away to comfort him with his distant, innocent past.

In all of his films Welles uses this contrast between movement and stillness to embody the fragility of life, to compress the change of a lifetime or even of an age into a few vivid moments. Sometimes he reverses his usual method of injecting stillness into movement. The calm flow of events in *Ambersons*, for example, is broken by the lively sleigh-riding sequence, its liveliness sharpened by the brightness of the snow and the airy rapidity of Bernard Herrmann's music. The sudden release of movement gives a physical reality to the passing of time.

Falstaff is one gigantic contrast of this kind. Its opening and closing scenes form a reflective prologue and epilogue that stand apart from the main action. The epilogue is straightforward: it shows Falstaff's bulky coffin being trundled slowly off into the distance. The prologue is more unusual. To create it, Welles has sliced half a dozen lines out of the middle of the scene in which Shallow summons potential recruits for Falstaff (*Henry IV, Part II, Act III*, scene ii). In these few lines Falstaff and Shallow reminisce about their youth. "We have heard the chimes at midnight, Master Shallow." "That we have, that we have. . . . Jesus, the days that we have seen!" Singled out in this way, the brief exchange carries a more powerful charge of nostalgia than in the scene as Shakespeare wrote it; and since the main action of the film is appended to the prologue like a huge flashback, this nostalgia affects everything that follows. Indeed, Welles has left the time and place of the prologue so vague that one may end up linking it with the epilogue, as if Falstaff and Shallow are viewing the past from some limbo outside time.

Seen in this context, such excesses of agitation as the battle scenes are only minor flaws. They do not in any way undermine the total effect of the film, of action embedded in reflection. As to other apparent excesses, they turn out to be no excesses at all. The vastness of the film's spaces serve to deepen the sense of nostalgia. The tavern, for example, is enlarged beyond probability in much the same way that a childhood haunt is enlarged in one's memory: this is how Falstaff, the perpetual child, would remember it. Similarly, the wide horizons of the film's outdoor scenes (actually shot in Spain) evoke the spacious, innocent Olde Englande that Falstaff imagined he lived in. Naturalistic settings would have called attention to the costumes, the archaic language, the theatrical structure of the scenes, everything except what's really important—the characters and their changing world. Welles's exaggerations give the film its human perspective.

Though nostalgia for lost innocence recurs in all the films, in none except *Arkadin* is there any sense of Welles repeating himself. Endless variations on his basic theme are possible, and Welles remains receptive to any or all of them. This is where his other Barnum characteristics —from swaggering camera to tongue-in-cheek humor—come into play. They are usually a sign of the unexpected.

In *Kane,* for example, when Susan makes her operatic debut, the camera suddenly takes off into the flies until it comes to rest on two stagehands, one of whom expressively grasps his nose with thumb and forefinger. The scene is very funny, all the more so because Welles builds it up with the same kind of camerawork he uses elsewhere for serious purposes: the long upward movement apes Kane's inordinate efforts to launch Susan's feeble talent. An even briefer example of this double-edged humor occurs in *Falstaff* when Sir John is lying supine on the tavern floor and Doll Tearsheet, coming to comfort him, climbs over his belly to reach his face. In one stroke Welles translates a Shakespearian metaphor into literal terms ("a mountain of flesh") and draws both humor and poignancy out of this new slant on Falstaff's fatness.

Welles's ability to bring out the unexpected in things usually taken for granted is at work throughout his best films. The most obvious example is found in the opposition between old and new in *Ambersons.* George, who stands for the innocent age that is dying, is the film's most objectionable character; Gene Morgan, who is helping create the age of noise and crowds and air pollution, is its most likable.

Characters like Kane and Quinlan gain depth from similar contradictions. Here, though, Welles avoids not only the obvious cliché of making them out-and-out monsters but [also] the less obvious cliché of making them sympathetic monsters. They do not arouse any set pattern of responses.

One's feelings about Kane, for example, change continually from repulsion to pity, indignation to amusement. At the point where Kane is running for governor and Boss Gettys summons Kane's wife to Susan's apartment with intent to blackmail, one is generally sympathetic to Kane. But in this scene, unexpectedly, it is Gettys who behaves with dignity, and one's sympathies switch from Kane to him. Welles accomplishes the switch without trickery: Kane behaves completely in character, and there is no suggestion that Gettys is a decent politician or has a heart of gold.

The cross-currents in *Touch of Evil* are even more complex, though at first sight they do not seem so: Vargas is likable and right, Quinlan is repulsive and wrong. But it so happens that Quinlan is right about

Sanchez's guilt (as he was no doubt right about many he framed in the past), which means that the moral issue between him and Vargas is not at all neat and abstract—it pivots on the possibility that a callous murderer may not only get away with his crime but his victim's daughter and wealth, too. Moreover, despite Vargas's moral stand, he is teetering on the same brink that Quinlan stepped over decades before, when his wife's murderer escaped punishment for lack of evidence. As soon as Vargas learns that his own wife has been abducted he too takes the law into his own hands. "I'm not a police officer, I'm a husband!" he shouts in the bar where Grandi's gang hangs out, and when they refuse to tell him anything he tries to beat the information out of them. It is only a touch of evil indeed that separates his destiny from Quinlan's.[2]

Welles's gift for making a vivid point with some unexpected development is at work even in the minor characters of *Touch of Evil*. Two of these, in particular, are involved in the moral issue—or rather, represent the kind of bystanders who try to avoid getting involved. The night man at the motel where Susan Vargas is being held prisoner is a weak, neurotic creature, so outraged at the slightest infringement on what he considers to be his rights that he has no thought to spare for anyone else's rights. In most films he would merely be contemptible; Welles makes him hilarious and unforgettable. Then there is the blind woman in the store where Vargas phones his wife. As he talks, the woman stands utterly still beside a sign that reads: "If you are mean enough to steal from the blind, go ahead." The scene arouses no sympathy for the woman but a sense of unease. The impression is that she is trading on her helplessness, refusing to take the slightest responsibility for what other people may do.

Perhaps the most subtly unexpected relationships in any of Welles's films are found in *Falstaff*. As portrayed by Shakespeare, Falstaff is not only lazy, gluttonous, cowardly, lecherous, dishonest, and the rest but also a great innocent. He is devoid of malice or calculation; no matter what is done to him, he remains open and trusting. He lives in a dream world where there are no politicians or policemen or pedagogues; and when Hal destroys that world by rejecting him, he does not adjust to reality but dies.

Welles magnifies this innocence both by uniting the Falstaff scenes from several plays and by establishing the strong mood of nostalgia discussed earlier. But—and this is the unexpected stroke—he does not

---

[2] In the novel from which Welles adapted the film, *Badge of Evil* by Whit Masterson, the framed man is innocent and there is nothing to explain why the police officer ever started framing suspects. These touches are Welles's own.

do this at Hal's expense. Even in the two parts of *Henry IV* as Shakespeare wrote them—and as they are usually produced on stage—it is hard not to take a dislike to Hal for his callousness and calculation. But Welles makes it as difficult as he can for the audience to take sides between Hal and Falstaff—or rather, to take one side and stick to it throughout.

In the film, Hal is at his least likable right at the beginning, even before the asides in which he talks of one day renouncing Falstaff's companionship. Welles presents him as an insecure, somewhat unstable, somewhat untrustworthy-looking youth, combining the flaws of immaturity with the shifty traits of his father.[3] Then, little by little, he acquires firmness and stature. The turning point comes on the battlefield at Shrewsbury. While King Henry is parleying with the rebel Worcester, Hal and Falstaff stand listening side by side. But their reactions are very different: Falstaff tosses out a frivolous remark; Hal silences him with a quiet "Peace, chewet, peace!" and walks over to join his father. During the battle itself, Hal emerges suddenly in close-up from a cloud of dust and is seen for the first time wearing his Prince of Wales coat of arms. From now on he is more and more the political-minded Prince Henry, less and less the irresponsible Hal. But because Welles has made him develop into a more likable human being at the same time that he has assumed his impersonal role, the prince manages to appear reasonable and humane even in the final confrontation with Falstaff: "I know thee not, old man. Fall to thy prayers. How ill white hairs become a fool and jester!"

Like Gene Morgan in *Ambersons,* Hal is changing the world for both better and worse. His political techniques, which Shakespeare depicts more fully in *Henry V,* will lead to Maoism and McCarthyism, but they will also lead to honest and efficient government. While the mood of the film is in sympathy with Falstaff, Welles makes it clear that there can be no final choice between Falstaff's anarchic freedom and Hal's well-ordered conformity.

The struggle between tradition and progress, old and new, order and disorder is one of the most powerful forces behind Welles's work. It is reflected in his American background and his love of Europe, and in his filmmaking that embraces both Shakespeare and modern American thrillers.

This drive to reconcile the irreconcilable goes beyond the subjects

---

[3] According to Shakespeare, Henry IV acquired the crown by force and duplicity. The subtlety of Hal's characterization—interpreted superbly by Keith Baxter—is obscured a little by John Gielgud's misreading of Henry. While the king has mellowed and weakened with age, he would never suggest—as Gielgud's plaintive declamation does—that the crown was thrust on him.

and themes of his films. In his European-made films it is at work even in the casting, which almost seems to be done on the assumption that Europe is a single country. The entire shaping of each film from *Kane* through *Falstaff* shows a desire to burst out of commonly accepted limitations. Welles is not content with a single viewpoint—in *Kane* there are at least seven different ones (the reminiscences of the five people interviewed by the reporter, the newsreel, and the God's-eye-view opening and closing scenes), while in all his films he alternates between the detachment of stationary long shots and the involvement of wide-angle close-ups or of dolly shots that stalk the action like a hungry leopard. He is not content with the straightforward flow of time—four of his films (*Kane, Othello, Arkadin, Falstaff*) begin with the end of the action before leaping to the beginning, and *Kane* continues leaping throughout; *Ambersons* frequently skips across the years with the most laconic of vignettes. In *Touch of Evil* and *The Trial* the leaps are not so much in time as in space.

The same drive makes itself felt in almost every aspect of Welles's style. It is found not only in the contrast between successive scenes—from stillness to movement, as described earlier, or from silence to noise, darkness to light, and so on—but also within individual scenes, many of which contain visual extremes or discords that threaten to burst the frame. Welles is continually using a wide-angle lens to throw a gulf between foreground and background, making figures near the camera loom preternaturally large over those further away. There are more unusual optical devices: the paperweight that falls from Kane's dying hand, covering and distorting half of the image; the hall of mirrors in *Lady from Shanghai*, splintering the screen into a dozen images; the magnifying glass that enlarges the flea trainer's eye in *Arkadin*. In other scenes the splintering is done by highlight and shadow: the reporter gesturing in the projector beam in *Kane*; Macbeth's breastplate highlighted, the rest of him in deep shadow after his "Tomorrow, and tomorrow, and tomorrow" soliloquy; the silhouetted funeral procession in *Othello*; the zebra stripes of light and dark that fall on Joseph K as he runs out of Titorelli's studio.

Welles's persistent attempts to harness opposites and contradictions generate a tremendous potential energy in his films. Usually this energy is released little by little, like a controlled nuclear reaction, maintaining a steady urgency that compels attention. But even his most controlled films are often on the verge of exploding. The three Shakespeare films, for example, suffer in varying degrees from inconsistency of acting styles and accents. The French accents of Jeanne Moreau as Doll Tearsheet and Marina Vlady as Lady Percy in *Falstaff* are the most egregious, but the roles are not central. More damage is done by Margaret Rutherford's assumed Irish accent as Mistress Quickly, since it reduces her description of Falstaff's death to a flat, self-conscious recitation; but Welles immediately repairs the damage in the touching epilogue of Falstaff's coffin.

The two biggest casualties of Welles's explosive pressure are *Arkadin* and *The Trial*. *Arkadin* is like a grenade that flies apart chiefly along its groovings: each episode holds together fairly well, but fails to connect with the others. *The Trial* is more like the nuclear explosion with which it ends: nearly everything in it disintegrates.

All the centripetal elements of Welles are present in force in *The Trial*. The repeated use of an extreme wide-angle lens exaggerates the depth of each scene, which is further splintered by the application of chiaroscuro to complex settings (the halls and catwalks of the law offices; Hastler's candle-dotted apartment; the cathedral). There are abrupt leaps in space and time not only from episode to episode but frequently from scene to scene. Both the cast and the locations are multinational.

Even the style and mood of the film come in fragments. Much of the decor derives from German expressionism of the 1920s, as do the *Metropolis*-like scenes in the vast office where Joseph K works and the rows of bare-chested accused waiting outside the law courts. The opening scenes in Joseph K's room are more like Hitchcock of the *Rope* period. The scene with Leni and Block in Hastler's kitchen (filmed partly with a long-focus lens) have a quiet hallucinatory quality reminiscent of *Last Year at Marienbad*.

The idea of continually changing the settings and mood of the film sounds as if it might have created an apt sense of unease, keeping the audience in the same off-balance frame of mind as Joseph K. Occasionally it does work like that. There is one superb example when K first visits the law courts and walks from a deserted corridor into a jam-packed courtroom. Welles intensifies the transition by having everyone rise to their feet as K enters, and the noise of their movement bursts into the silence like a menacing roar. (This is Welles's own addition— in Kafka's book no one in the courtroom takes any notice of K.)

Most of the transitions, however, break the tension instead of heightening it. The varied settings do not fuse together into an eerie world of their own but remain obstinately separate. Thus when K walks from the huge office into the storeroom where the policemen are being punished, the agoraphobic size of the former and the claustrophobic darkness of the latter tend not to reinforce but to neutralize each other. Time and time again in the film the nightmare is short-circuited.

To explain the failure of *The Trial* it's easy to fall back on the accusation of size and showiness. It's easy to argue that Welles's style is too florid for Kafka, who relied on restraint to convey the bizarre misadventures of Joseph K. But these criticisms are irrelevant because they can be leveled at Welles's other films which do not fall to pieces.

Consider *Othello,* which has just as many reasons as *The Trial* for disintegrating. Much of the film leaps from place to place with no regard for topographical continuity: any attempt to visualize the interior layout of Othello's castle is quite pointless. As with *The Trial,* Welles in adapting the original shifts some scenes and alters others (such as the extended bathhouse scene where Iago kills Roderigo). He breaks up the rhythms of Shakespeare's play, sometimes accelerating, sometimes almost halting the action. The settings and the cast are multinational. Most disruptive of all, his work on the film continued on and off for a period of three years.

Yet the film translates Shakespeare into screen terms with a superb coherence. Welles sets the whole tragedy in perspective with an opening sequence that interweaves the funeral corteges of Othello and Desdemona and the dragging of Iago to his punishment. In contrast to the sweeping flow of these scenes, the beginning of the action has a staccato rhythm as Iago and Roderigo follow Othello and Desdemona to their wedding and then rouse Brabantio. Calm is restored when Othello comes to justify his marrying Desdemona. But from this point on the staccato rhythm associated with Iago gradually imposes itself on Othello's stately rhythm, and the increasing complexity of the film's movements suggests the increasing turmoil of doubt in Othello's mind. In the death scene, when Othello has finally decided there *is* no doubt of Desdemona's infidelity, the stately rhythm reasserts itself. Then there is a brief flurry of movement as Iago's duplicity is exposed and Othello kills himself, followed by a reprise of the grave calm of the opening scene.

There is only one moment, near the end of the film, where the disintegrating forces win out. Welles has Othello stab himself before instead of after the long speech in which he refers to himself as "one whose hand,/Like the base Indian, threw a pearl away/Richer than all his tribe." During part of the speech Othello strides across the hall toward Desdemona's body, and this rather improbable movement is intercut with a jarring close-up in which Welles has a Harry Lime–like smile on his face. This one lapse cannot spoil the film: it does, however, make one realize just how cohesive the rest of the film has been.

The binding force in *Othello* and in most of Welles's other films is his use of symbolism. Even the most explicit of Welles's symbols do not exist in isolation: they are rooted deep in the action of the film and share the same degree of reality.

Rosebud, for example, appears at first to be a pat and superficial symbol. As with all mysteries, its revelation is something of a letdown: the sled is "only" a symbol of Kane's childhood. But the symbolism is not confined to the object itself. In fact, the adult Kane is never seen looking at it—the word Rosebud is triggered by the sight of Susan's paperweight. But here again the symbolism goes beyond the object. The paperweight is not merely an artificial snow scene recalling a real one but a snow scene encapsulated and unattainable, like Kane's lost innocence. Moreover, when the paperweight appears in close-up Welles highlights it so that it takes on a glowing halation—very much like the glare of the stage lights when Susan makes her operatic debut. Kane drives Susan to her vocal disaster not just to show his power but because, his own desire being unattainable, he wants hers to come true. Susan fails—the ironic floodlight flickers out as her voice trails away—and she is able to come to terms with reality. But the glow of Kane's desire continues to the end: the paperweight falls and smashes only after his death.

There are further ramifications to this symbolism. When the paperweight is shaken, its artificial snow settles again with preternatural slowness, prolonging and intensifying the matter-of-fact snowfall that covers the sled after young Kane leaves home. This slow settling, which is paralleled in the lingering dissolves between the reporter's interviews and his interviewees' reminiscences, suggests not only the loss of Kane's childhood innocence but the loss of all things with the relentless flow of time. At the end of the film Welles brings out this wider implication still more powerfully by accelerating the time effect. The whole of Kane's life is compressed symbolically into a few seconds as the sled —his childhood reality and manhood dream—burns and dissolves into smoke.

I'm not implying that Welles consciously planned all these interrelationships. But I do believe that he chose the particular objects, incidents, and techniques in these scenes because they felt right to him— and they felt right because they connected with the underlying symbolism. Anyone who thinks my analysis is far-fetched should try to explain why the burning of Rosebud is such a powerful scene—even more powerful than the book-burning scenes in *Fahrenheit 451*. After all, a sled lacks the ready-made associations that books have; and Rosebud is not even a new and handsome object like Dali's *Secret Life*, over whose destruction Truffaut lingers for the longest time. It is the interlinking of symbols beneath the surface of *Kane* that accumulates the power of the final scenes.

This symbolism underlying conspicuous symbols can be found in nearly all of Welles's films. Anyone who's seen *The Lady from Shanghai* will remember the squid that pulses up and down in the aquarium as Mike and Elsa kiss. In isolation this might be an overemphatic comment on Elsa's predatory nature, but it works because Welles has imbued the whole film with visual and verbal imagery of the sea. The

Lady herself comes from one seaport and has settled in another (San Francisco), and many scenes take place on or by the water. The squid is one of several images involving dangers that lurk beneath the surface, just as they lurk behind Elsa's alluring exterior: there are shots of a water snake and an alligator, and Mike relates a parable about sharks that destroy one another. Even the hall of mirrors connects with the pelagic imagery: the multiple reflections are like waves receding row after row, and when the mirrors are smashed Mike can finally step out onto terra firma, ignoring Elsa's last siren call. It is this cumulative imagery that helps place *The Lady from Shanghai* above other superior thrillers, which owe their success either to a series of disparate effects (like *The Wages of Fear*) or to sheer verve (like *The Big Sleep*).

The binding symbolism of *Othello* is also based on a sea-to-land progression, but Welles develops it far more subtly than in *The Lady from Shanghai* and with a totally different meaning. Othello is a naval general and water is his element. At the beginning of the film, when he is strong and self-assured, he glides with Desdemona in a gondola, he commands a warship on the billowy sea, he strides beneath pennants that flutter in a stiff sea breeze. Then, as doubts about Desdemona grow in his mind, he begins to flounder out of his element. The one really spectacular scene in the film shows this transition with extraordinary vividness. When Iago says that Cassio has talked of having slept with Desdemona, Othello staggers away (Shakespeare's stage direction reads that he "falls in a trance") and finds himself lying on the waterfront beneath a parapet from which a row of people stare down at him. Welles uses a wide-angle lens and places Othello's bemused face in close-up so that it completely dwarfs the figures above: it is as if Othello were a beached whale. In more and more of the later scenes Welles draws the action away from the sea and the open air to keep Othello stranded. And in these interior scenes he leaves the walls and floors as bare as possible, criss-crossing them with spikes of shadow, in order to accentuate their dryness and airlessness.

In films with fewer centrifugal pressures than *Othello* or *Kane* the underlying symbolism plays a less important role. Indeed, it may merge indistinguishably into style: the leisurely movement of *Ambersons* and the vast spaces of *Falstaff* might be described as both medium and message.

Elsewhere the symbolism may be too rigid for the theme, or the theme too weak for the symbolism. *Macbeth* is conceived in terms of darkness, which is appropriate enough, but the darkness hardly varies: the film consists of one low-key scene after another. There is no vivid impression of Macbeth sinking from innocence into evil and despair as there is of Othello sinking from innocence into anguish. In *The Stranger* Welles does oppose darkness with light, as the film alternates between the shadowy belfry where Frank Kindler tinkers with the church clock and the whiteness of the New England colonial buildings. But here the situation is too static: the Nazi war criminal pretending to be a good small-town citizen is unchangingly evil all along.

Arkadin fails because its symbolism doesn't counteract but reinforces the centrifugal pressures. In order to suggest the multiple layers of Arkadin's personality, Welles locates the film in different elements—land, sea, air—and in different climates, from the sunny Mediterranean to wintry Germany. But the symbolism lacks a second layer of its own that would bind this geographic diversity together.

As to *The Trial*, it has no underlying symbolism whatsoever—all its symbolism is on the surface. The trouble is not so much that Welles departs from the book but that he does not depart far enough. In the book, Kafka grafts bizarre scenes onto the everyday settings of Prague, binding them together with a matter-of-fact style of writing. But it is impossible to film the scenes as Kafka describes them and at the same time remain matter-of-fact. For example, Kafka can casually write that "the size of the Cathedral struck him as bordering on the limit of what human beings could bear," but this scene cannot be filmed with anything approaching casualness. In adapting the book for the screen Welles had two choices: to tone down Kafka's incidents until they could plausibly fit the everyday settings of a real city, or to amplify Kafka's settings until they fitted the bizarre incidents. The latter choice, arguably the more faithful, was the one Welles made; and he amplifies the style along with the settings.

In making this choice, however, Welles cut himself off from a prime source of strength. *The Trial* is the only one of his films that is not rooted in reality. The best films are worlds of their own that touch common experience at enough points to be accepted as reflections of the real world. It is this basis of reality that sustains Welles's underlying symbolism, which is nearly always elemental in nature—images of air, water, snow, fire, light, darkness.

The Trial is not one world but a succession of different worlds. Many of the scenes are so dissimilar in location, tempo, and atmosphere that it is hardly possible to imagine them coexisting on any plane of reality. Weather, the progression of night and day, natural processes of all kinds are almost completely eliminated. There is nothing for any elemental symbolism to get a grip on.

It may be argued that *The Trial* is not meant to be coherent like Welles's other films for the simple reason that it is portraying an incoherent world—that by basing the style of this film on loose ends and nonsequiturs, Welles conveys the sharpest possible sense of the menacing absurdity of modern life. This is all very plausible and could lead to long and inconclusive discussion about the merits of portraying incoherence incoherently, boredom boringly, and so on. Luckily Welles has provided his own standard of comparison in *Touch of Evil*, which portrays the incoherence of modern life with a remarkable coherence of style and symbolism.

This is a film of darkness. It begins and ends in the night, and there are many other nocturnal or twilit scenes in between. But it is not a montonously dark film like *Macbeth*. The night is punctuated throughout with lights that make the darkness more menacing, from the glare of the exploding car to the pulsing of neon signs.

It is in this mechanical pulsing rather than in the light and darkness themselves that the underlying symbolism is to be found. *Touch of Evil* is geared to the automatic machinery of our time. The film opens with a close-up of the time bomb as it is set to tick its way to destruction. The film ends with Quinlan unwittingly confessing to a tape recorder. The two machines are uncannily similar in appearance—and also in effect, since the recorder in its own way destroys Quinlan as thoroughly as any bomb.

In between these two mechanical destroyers, other machines dominate the action. In the famous three-minute opening scene the camera follows the car but never allows a clear glimpse of the man and woman riding in it. When Susan Vargas stands on the hotel fire escape calling for help, the engine of Vargas's car drowns out her voice and he speeds unknowingly past her. Quinlan's car is his alter ego: it is big and fat (and Welles exaggerates its fatness with the wide-angle lens), and when it lurches across the quarrying site where the dynamite was stolen it translates Quinlan's lazy ruthlessness into action. In a way, Quinlan himself is a machine—he has lost nearly all of his human flexibility in order to become an efficient manufacturer of convicted criminals. In the final scene his voice is heard alternately from the radio pick-up and direct from his mouth, as if there were little difference between the two sources; while all around him the oil wells pump on and on in a monstrous parody of his obsession.

Though Quinlan is the only character who has succumbed to the temptation of being a machine, nearly everyone in the film is under pressure to do so. Action, dialogue, camera movement, and editing conspire to keep the film rolling onward with machine-like relentlessness. Characters are caught up in this tremendous momentum in much the same way that Joseph K is caught up in the legal labyrinth of *The Trial*: the important difference is that the momentum of *Touch of Evil* is not conveyed indirectly through fantasy but as a direct, tangible force.

A few of the characters avoid being caught up in the momentum—

at a price. Tanya and the blind store woman choose to be bystanders in life. The night clerk at the motel is outraged to find himself in a situation that requires positive action. The scenes involving each of these three have an unexpected spaciousness that heightens the ruthless urgency of the rest of the film.

It is the character who accepts the greatest responsibility, Vargas, who runs the greatest risk of succumbing to the machines. The time bomb at the beginning of the film is in the hands of a murderer; the recorder at the end is in Vargas's hands. There is no doubt that Vargas is right to destroy Quinlan; but the film leaves the audience to wonder whether in so doing Vargas has begun to destroy himself.

I don't want to overpraise *Touch of Evil*. For all its richness it remains a thriller with a Hollywood hero.[4] But it does succeed superbly where *The Trial* fails—in revealing a nightmare world behind everyday reality.

Moreover, in *Touch of Evil* Welles is once again several years ahead of his time. It is only in the sixties that filmmakers have really assimilated the effects of post–World War II technological development on everyday life. Before then technology was usually featured either as mere decor or (in its noisier and uglier manifestations) as the antithesis to a quiet upper-income semirural existence. Welles makes it an integral part of life, and though he also uses it to symbolize the temptation of evil he certainly does not present it as the cause. In this, *Touch of Evil* anticipates Truffaut's approach to gadgetry in *The Soft Skin* and, more indirectly, Godard's in *The Married Woman*. It's also worth noting that a 1967 film like Furie's *The Naked Runner*, which links modern gadgetry to the amoral expedients of espionage, says nothing that *Touch of Evil* didn't say far better and far less pretentiously ten years before.

It may seem a measure of Welles's limitations that his Hollywood-made *Touch of Evil* is better than his independently made *Trial*. But his work resists easy generalizations. Each of his really outstanding films—*Kane, Ambersons, Othello,* and *Touch of Evil,* with *Falstaff* as a close runner-up—was made under very different conditions. If his most independent film is a failure, it may well be because he seized the opportunity to take bigger risks.

In every one of his films Welles has taken some kind of risk. He has always been willing to pit his recurring theme of lost innocence and his elemental symbolism against the explosive diversity of his other resources. His films depend for their success on a fine balance of all kinds of opposites—sophistication and simplicity, realism and expres-

---

[4] Even though Charlton Heston plays Vargas well, the mere fact that he is a star suggests that Vargas is unequivocally in the right.

sionism, introversion and extroversion, clarity and confusion. And yet, with each film, he has rejected the cautiousness and calculation that could assure him of balance at the expense of richness and resonance. He himself has never lost all of the innocence with which he first tackled *Kane*.

REVIEWS

JOHN O'HARA

It is with exceeding regret that your faithful bystander reports that he has just seen a picture which he thinks must be the best picture he ever saw.

With no less regret he reports that he has just seen the best actor in the history of acting.

Name of picture: *Citizen Kane.*
Name of actor: Orson Welles.
Reason for regret: you, my dear, may never see the picture.
(From now on, it's *I*.)

I saw *Citizen Kane* the other night. I am told that my name was crossed off a list of persons who were invited to look at the picture, my name being crossed off because some big shot remembered I had been a newspaperman. So, for the first time in my life, I indignantly denied I was a newspaperman. Nevertheless, I had to be snuck into the showing of *Citizen Kane* under a phony name. That's what's going on about this wonderful picture. Intrigue.

Why intrigue? Well, because. A few obsequious and/or bulbous middle-aged ladies think the picture ought not to be shown, owing to the fact that the picture is rumored to have something to do with a certain publisher, who, for the first time in his life, or maybe the second, shall be nameless. That the nameless publisher might be astute enough to realize that for the first time in his rowdy life he had been made a human being did not worry the loyal ladies. Sycophancy of that kind, like curtseying, is deliberate. The ladies merely wait for a chance to show they can still do it, even if it means cracking a femur. This time I think they may have cracked off more than they can chew. I hope.

The story is that of a publisher, from his whippersnapper to his doting days. His origin is humble, and most likely not acceptable to the quarreling ladies, whose origin is not for a second in question here.

From Newsweek Magazine *13 (March 1941): 60. Reprinted by permission of* Newsweek Magazine.

A fresh punk out of various colleges, the publisher walks into a newspaper office as a not quite legitimate heir, and thereupon enjoys himself and power. At a rather late date it is shown that his sybaritic pastimes and his power are incomplete, for he can buy or produce everything but love. He doesn't give love; he lacks love. With everything in the world that you and I might expect to bring happiness, the publisher is a lonely, unwanted, feared, tragicomic man. He dies, speaking one mysterious word, a female name. At the end of this wonderful picture you get to know what the name was. You also (later) realize how silly women can be, especially obsequious women.

Look in vain here for any but obscure hints as to the story of *Citizen Kane*. My intention is to make you want to see the picture; if possible, to make you wonder why you are not seeing what I think is as good a picture as was ever made. Up to now I have thought that the very best talking picture ever made was *M*. I have seen *M* at least eight times. As a movie writer and press agent I used to have them run off the attack sequence in *The Big Parade,* the one in the woods where the boys don't know where the sharpshooter's going to hit next, everytime I had a chance. One of my very favorite silents was that beautiful job *The Great Gatsby*. And if you want to settle bets on any phase of *The Birth of a Nation,* call me. But *Citizen Kane* is Late 1941. It lacks nothing.

And aside from what it does not lack, *Citizen Kane* has Orson Welles. It is traditional that if you are a great artist, no one gives a damn about you while you're still alive. Welles has had plenty of that. He got a tag put to his name through the Mars thing, just as Scott Fitzgerald, who wrote better than any man in our time, got a Jazz Age tag put to his name. I say, if you plan to have any grandchildren to see and to bore, see Orson Welles so that you can bore your grandchildren with some honesty. There never has been a better actor than Orson Welles. I just got finished saying there never has been a better actor than Orson Welles, and I don't want any of your lip.

Do yourself a favor. Go to your neighborhood exhibitor and ask him why he isn't showing *Citizen Kane. Then* sue me.

BOSLEY CROWTHER

(MAY 2, 1941)

Within the withering spotlight as no other film has ever been before, Orson Welles's *Citizen Kane* had its world première at the Palace last evening. And now that the wraps are off, the mystery has been exposed, and Mr. Welles and the RKO directors have taken the much-debated leap, it can be safely stated that suppression of this film would have been a crime. For, in spite of some disconcerting lapses and strange ambiguities in the creation of the principal character, *Citizen Kane* is far and away the most surprising and cinematically exciting motion picture to be seen here in many a moon. As a matter of fact, it comes close to being the most sensational film ever made in Hollywood.

Count on Mr. Welles; he doesn't do things by halves. Being a mercurial fellow, with a frightening theatrical flair, he moved right into the movies, grabbed the medium by the ears and began to toss it around with the dexterity of a seasoned veteran. Fact is, he handled it with more verve and inspired ingenuity than any of the elder craftsmen have exhibited in years. With the able assistance of Gregg Toland, whose services should not be overlooked, he found in the camera the perfect instrument to encompass his dramatic energies and absorb his prolific ideas. Upon the screen he discovered an area large enough for his expansive whims to have free play. And the consequence is that he has made a picture of tremendous and overpowering scope, not in physical extent so much as in its rapid and graphic rotation of thoughts. Mr. Welles has put upon the screen a motion picture that really moves.

As for the story which he tells—and which has provoked such an uncommon fuss—this corner frankly holds considerable reservation. Naturally we wouldn't know how closely—if at all—it parallels the life of an eminent publisher, as has been somewhat cryptically alleged. But that is beside the point in a rigidly critical appraisal. The blamable

From The New York Times (*May 2, 1941 and May 4, 1941*). *Copyright © 1941 by The New York Times Company. Reprinted by permission of* The New York Times.

circumstance is that it fails to provide a clear picture of the character and motives behind the man about whom the whole thing revolves.

As the picture opens, Charles Kane lies dying in the fabulous castle he has built—the castle called Xanadu, in which he has surrounded himself with vast treasures. And as death closes his eyes his heavy lips murmur one word, "Rosebud." Suddenly the death scene is broken; the screen becomes alive with a staccato March-of-Time-like news feature recounting the career of the dead man—how, as a poor boy, he came into great wealth, how he became a newspaper publisher as a young man, how he aspired to political office, was defeated because of a personal scandal, devoted himself to material acquisition and finally died.

But the editor of the news feature is not satisfied; he wants to know the secret of Kane's strange nature and especially what he meant by "Rosebud." So a reporter is dispatched to find out, and the remainder of the picture is devoted to an absorbing visualization of Kane's phenomenal career as told by his boyhood guardian, two of his closest newspaper associates, and his mistress. Each is agreed on one thing —that Kane was a titanic egomaniac. It is also clearly revealed that the man was in some way consumed by his own terrifying selfishness. But just exactly what it is that eats upon him, why it is there and, for that matter, whether Kane is really a villain, a social parasite, is never clearly revealed. And the final, poignant identification of "Rosebud" sheds little more than a vague, sentimental light upon his character. At the end Kubla Kane is still an enigma—a very confusing one.

But check that off to the absorption of Mr. Welles in more visible details. Like the novelist, Thomas Wolfe, his abundance of imagery is so great that it sometimes gets in the way of his logic. And the less critical will probably be content with an undefined Kane, anyhow. After all, nobody understood him. Why should Mr. Welles? Isn't it enough that he presents a theatrical character with consummate theatricality?

We would, indeed, like to say as many nice things as possible about everything else in this film—about the excellent direction of Mr. Welles, about the sure and penetrating performances of literally every member of the cast and about the stunning manner in which the music of Bernard Herrmann has been used. Space, unfortunately, is short. All we can say, in conclusion, is that you shouldn't miss this film. It is cynical, ironic, sometimes oppressive, and as realistic as a slap. But it has more vitality than fifteen other films we could name. And, although it may not give a thoroughly clear answer, at least it brings to mind one deeply moral thought: For what shall it profit a man if he shall gain the whole world and lose his own soul? See *Citizen Kane* for further details.

(MAY 4, 1941)

Now that the returns are in from most of the local journalistic precincts and Orson Welles's *Citizen Kane* has been overwhelmingly selected as one of the great (if not the greatest) motion pictures of all time, this department rather finds itself with the uncomfortable feeling of a cat regarding a king. For we, in spite of the fact that we cast our vote in favor of it, frankly went to the polls with our fingers dextrously crossed and came away vaguely uneasy about the absolute wisdom of the choice. Mr. Welles has made an absorbing, exciting motion picture, and there is no question but what, compared with the average, it is vastly superior. But is it, as some of the more enthusiastic votecasters have called it, the greatest film ever made? Is it, indeed, a great picture—saying "great" with awe in one's voice? And does it promise much for the future of its amazing young producer? We, a minority feline, are not altogether certain, and a careful consideration of those questions will form the burden of these allegedly second thoughts.

One fact cannot be disregarded in an estimation of this film: when *Citizen Kane* had its world première at the Palace on Thursday evening it was riding the crest of perhaps the most provocative publicity wave ever to float a motion picture. The circumstances of the case are too familiar for more than capsule repetition. Mr. Welles had made the picture in the greatest secrecy—had written it, produced it, directed it, and acted in it with carte blanche from RKO, his apparently self-satisfied sponsor. Furthermore, the aura of mystery was rendered even more formidable by the fact that Mr. Welles was an enfant terrible of note, had created quite a murmur with his well-advertised oddities and had already taken a bye on two previously projected films.

Then suddenly the word got around as to what *Citizen Kane* was all about—the story of a newspaper publisher who rules a chain of aggressive journals and lives in baronial splendor surrounded by treasures of art. Immediately folks got suspicious that it might bear a close parallel to the life of an eminent publisher now living in much the same way. Certain ones saw the picture and allegedly pulled strings to have it squelched. The matter at once became news. Would *Citizen Kane* be released? Would RKO dare to fly in the face of assumed improvidence? Many folks became considerably disturbed, so when finally the picture was presented it had an audience waiting breathless and alert.

This fact is very important for one particular reason: regardless of what the film actually showed upon the screen, this extraordinary advance publicity preordered a mental attitude. Folks who are generally familiar with the history of yellow journalism in America and with its more notorious exponents were prepared to see in *Citizen Kane* an archetype of ruthless publisher. Further, they were ready to respond with quick and prescient recognition to even the slightest implication. And although the film fails completely to state a case against Publisher Kane, to identify him except by vague suggestion with the flagrant tactics of yellow journalists, it is the belief of this department that most of the people who have seen the picture so far have come away with the solid conviction that they have beheld the image of an unscrupulous tycoon.

Yet at no point in the picture is a black mark actually checked against Kane. Not a shred of evidence is presented to indicate absolutely that he is a social scoundrel. As a matter of fact, there is no reason to assume from what is shown upon the screen that he is anything but an honest publisher with a consistently conscientious attitude toward society. This is a surprising realization after you've seen the film, but it is a fact. We saw it twice just to make sure. And because there is this lack of positive characterization, because the real significance of Kane depends entirely upon one's personal preconceptions, we are inclined to feel that Mr. Welles is slightly hoodwinking the public. Or rather, we should say that circumstances have made it possible for him to do so.

Of course one might reasonably argue that Mr. Welles, as an expert showman, has simply taken advantage of an established attitude and that the picture anyhow is not concerned so much with the importance of Kane to society as it is with the importance of the man to himself. In a measure this is true. But the entire significance of Kane to himself and to those around him is predicated upon the assumption that he is a sort of monster, that he has betrayed everything that is decent in his mania for wealth and power. And this the picture does not show.

We hate to discover inconsistency in a film which is so beautifully made—and beautiful is a temperate word for Mr. Welles's *Citizen Kane*. Everything about it, from a technical point of view, is surpassingly magnificent. With the able assistance of Gregg Toland, whose contribution was obviously great, he has made use of all the best devices of pure cinema which have been brought out through the years. And he has invented a few of his own. Mr. Welles and Mr. Toland have used the camera not only to record a story but to comment upon it, to compose by visual contrasts and sharp glimpses caught from unusual points an overpoweringly suggestive film. The music of Bernard Herrmann is applied with incomparable effect; Mr. Welles has directed the whole with the sureness and distinction of a seasoned master, and the entire cast—but especially Joseph Cotten, Dorothy Comingore, Everett Sloane, and Mr. Welles himself—perform it in a manner which puts to shame the surface posturings of some of our more popular stars.

But this corner is inclined to suspect that the enthusiasm with which Mr. Welles made the film—the natural bent of a first-class showman toward eloquent and dramatic effects—rather worked against the logic of his story. And the accomplishment of his purpose has been so completely impressive that it tends to blind the audience to the holes in the fabric. . . . And when the significance of "Rosebud" is made apparent in the final sequence of the film, it provides little more than a dramatic and poignant shock. It does not clarify, except by sentimental suggestion, the reason for Kane's complexity.

And so we are bound to conclude that this picture is not truly great, for its theme is basically vague and its significance depends on circumstances. Unquestionably, Mr. Welles is the most dynamic newcomer in films and his talents are infinite. But the showman will have to acquire a good bit more discipline before he is thoroughly dependable. When he does—and let's hope it will be soon—his fame should extend to Mars.

OTIS FERGUSON

Citizen Kane can be approached in several ways: as a film, as an event, as a topic of the times, etc. The outline of the story is simplicity itself, almost like saying, "Once upon a time there was a man of whom certain things are remembered." But its presentation is managed in complex ways and its conclusions are so vague with the shadows of meaning that it is easy to read almost anything into it, including what was actually put there. The things to be said are that it is the boldest freehand stroke in major screen production since Griffith and Bitzer were running wild to unshackle the camera; that it has the excitement

From The New Republic *114* (June 2, 1941): 760–61. Reprinted by permission of Dorothy Chamberlain.

of all surprises without stirring emotions much more enduring; and that in the line of the narrative film, as developed in all countries but most highly on the West Coast of America, it holds no great place.

The picture starts right in with the death of Citizen Kane alone with his crates of priceless art treasures in his fabulous castle on a mountain, where he has ruled for a time at least a miniature of the world. He said a thing when he died and the March of Time wants to make a story out of it, so we start combing the file of old acquaintance, with episode by episode told in flashbacks, and eventually we get the answer through the efforts of the inquiring reporter, who tracks down documents, the man's oldest friend, his newspaper manager, the girl, the butler of the castle. Some of the points are made by the people questioned; some are made in what there is of story as it moves over the years from back to front; but the main point is that Citizen Kane wanted love from the world and went to most of his fantastic extremes to get it, yet never had any love of his own to give. And the thing the searchers have been after, the dying apostrophe which assumes the importance of a mystery-story clue in the last sequence, develops as no more than a memory of the self of his childhood.

There has been so much snarling and blowing on the subject of what this picture is about that it won't hurt to clear the issue: most of the surface facts parallel incidents in the career of one W. R. Hearst; some traits are borrowed from other figures; some are pure ad-libbing. But any resemblance is distinctly coincidental; I could, and would if the editor were not afraid of libel, give you quite a list of Hearst's undesirable characteristics not possessed by Kane. As for the importance of the figure as an element of society, I don't think you can make that stick either. Kane started a war to get circulation for his paper; we hear in casual reference that he is a yellow journalist and we see in a three-for-a-nickel montage clip that he fought graft and some corrupt trusts; there is a prophecy, not followed up, that when the workingman becomes organized labor he will not love the workingman; he is interviewed by the press and makes wild statements with gravity; when anyone gets in his way he calls him an anarchist. Otherwise his troubles are personal, and his death is that of a domineering and lonely man, known to all for his money, loved by none. The only possible moral of the picture is, don't be that way or you'll be sorry.

Beyond the facts of the career there is the man himself and this man is Orson Welles, young, older, middle-aged, and in the last decrepit years, dominant throughout. Here perhaps, not so much spoken as expressed in the figure and bearing, is the ruthless force, the self-will, the restless-acquisitive which we feel the story should express if it is to tell of these things at all. This man in these circumstances should be our twentieth-century brand of a figure out of Gustavus Myers: he did not roll up that fortune to start with, but he is no second generation gone to seed, for he turned the nonworking capital into influence and public excitement and a sort of twisted splendor. It is as though Welles, as the man who conceived and produced this film story, had little enough grasp of the issues involved; but Welles as the actor somehow managed, by the genius that is in actors when they have it, to be more of the thing than he could realize. His presence in the picture is always a vital thing, an object of fascination to the beholder. In fact, without him the picture would have fallen all into its various component pieces of effect, allusion and display. He is the big part and no one will say he is not worth it.

Of his actors, you can say that there are good jobs done and also that there are better ones still to be done. Dorothy Comingore is forced to be too shrill as the shrill wife (the audience ear will absorb only so much) and too ham as the opera singer (subtlety never hurt anyone, and those of us who aren't gaping yokels are not alone, Mr. Orson Citizen). Joseph Cotten had a part that was possibly short on savor because when he was with the great man he had to be something of a chump and when he was talking of him afterwards he had to be something of a Mr. Chips, with twinkle and lip-smacking. Ray Collins did a good piece of work with a stock part, and so did all the other stock parts; but to me the man to remember was Everett Sloane, who seemed to understand and seemed to represent it, the little man with the big mind, the projection without the face motion and flapping of arms. You may be surprised when you take the film apart, and find that his relations to any analysis of Kane were as much as anything else the things that made him real.

Now I believe we can look at the picture, and of course we have been told to wait for that. The picture. The new art. The camera unbound. The picture is very exciting to anyone who gets excited about how things can be done in the movies; and the many places where it takes off like the Wright brothers should be credited to Welles first and his cameraman second (Herman J. Mankiewicz as writing collaborator should come in too). The Kubla Khan setting, the electioneering stage, the end of the rough-cut in the Marsh of Thyme projection room, the kid outside the window in the legacy scene, the opera stage, the dramatics of the review copy on opening night—the whole idea of a man in these attitudes must be credited to Welles himself.

And in these things there is no doubt the picture is dramatic. But what goes on between the dramatic high points, the story? No. What goes on is talk and more talk. And while the stage may stand for this, the movies don't. And where a cameraman like Gregg Toland can be every sort of help to a director, in showing him what will pick up, in getting this effect or that, in achieving some lifting trick the guy has thought up, the cameraman still can't teach him how to shoot and cut a picture, even if he knows how himself. It is a thing that takes years and practice to learn. And its main problem always is story, story, story—or, How can we do it to them so they don't know beforehand that it's being done? Low-key photography won't help, except in the case of critics. Crane shots and pan shots, funny angles like showing the guy as though you were lying down at his feet, or moving in over him on the wings of an angel, won't help. Partial lighting won't help, or even blacking out a face or figure won't help, though it may keep people puzzled. Tricks and symbols never really come to much. The real art of movies concentrates on getting the right story and the right actors, the right kind of production and then smoothing everything out. And after that, in figuring how each idea can be made true, how each action can be made to happen, how you cut and reverse-camera and remake each minute of action, and run it into a line afterwards, like the motion in the ocean. Does this picture do this? See some future issue when I have the time to say it doesn't, quite. Right now I have to hurry to catch a boat back to New York.

CEDRIC BELFRAGE

Apparently *Citizen Kane* is not, after all, destined to go down in history as the great Hollywood myth. The press has seen it, with highballs, caviar, canapes, and soft music to follow—and never were these traditional cushioners of a flop's fall so superfluous. It is not difficult to imagine the tremendous forces that have been at grips behind the scenes to decide whether it should be shown or shelved. On the one hand, a picture which the people of America will pay millions of dollars to see. On the other, the might and majesty and profits of dark yellow journalism—exposed by *Kane* so effectively, because so humanly and with such inspired craftsmanship.

There has never—and I speak as one who has attended thousands of them—been a more exciting press show. For on that screen the

From The Clipper *1 (May 1941).*

slaves, the houris, and the camp-followers of the press lords saw some of the truth told about what enslaves, degrades, and makes prostitutes of them. And at the same time they saw the whole spangled pyramid of Hollywood movie conventions, which they had had to support with their bodies in their advertisement-controlled "criticism," toppled over and left in ruins by the heroic Orson Welles and his Mercury Theater nobodies.

Heaven knows what lies or evasions many of them had to go back to their offices and write about the picture's theme—for it is very much one of those assignments in which, as we delicately phrase it, "questions of policy" are involved. But never mind. The people are going to see *Citizen Kane*, and not one of them will *be quite the same person after seeing it as he was before*. It is as profoundly moving an experience as only this extraordinary and hitherto unexplored medium of sound-cinema can afford in two hours. You leave it with regret, wishing you could see it all through again, feeling all of your old belief in the medium restored, all of your shattered illusions made whole. You become dizzy trying to recall all the good things in it, the excellencies of different kinds—lighting, composition, direction, dialogue, acting, makeup, music and sound, editing and construction—which are present simultaneously at almost any moment in the picture. You realize how rusty your faculties for apprehending all the qualities of a motion picture have become, through long experience of striving to find even one good quality at a time.

Certainly it represents a revolution, and a major one, in Hollywood's approach to cinema. Trying to find in my critical memories any Hollywood celluloid that gave me a comparative emotional and artistic experience, I could only think of Chaplin's *Woman of Paris*. One recalls how the techniques used in that picture turned the studios upside down and inside out. Remember Edna Purviance waiting for the train which was to take her away from her home and her lover to Paris. She stood quite still, filling the screen, looking straight ahead of her just over the camera. The train was never shown except by shadows from its lights which passed, gradually slowing to a halt, over her face—then she walked toward the camera and out of the picture. Remember how the fact that she was being kept by Menjou in the Paris flat was shown simply by Menjou going to a drawer and taking a handkerchief —then a close-up of a collar dropping out. Simple and obvious, perhaps—but something nobody had ever done before; as exciting as the cross-cut simultaneous-action chase was in its day, and for the same reason, it was a use of the medium in an authentic way, giving it the dignity of being a medium different from the stage or any other, able to do things the others cannot do. Only the movie could in a few seconds emphasize that collar and what it meant, and so tell a whole story with it.

Since then sound has come. And one can fairly say that, if possibly there are a hundred uses of sound authentic and appropriate to the sound-film medium, at most one or two have been exploited by Hollywood. Perhaps of all the delectable flavors that linger on the palate after seeing *Kane,* the use of sound is strongest. Welles brings to the movie studio a mastery of sound technique in the radio medium, yet that mastery is such that it adapts itself to cinema with effortlessness and discrimination. The scene that everyone will be speaking about —that will be to sound-film what Chaplin's train scene was to silent-film—is the breakfast-table sequence between Kane and his first wife. The whole story of that marriage is told while they sit at the table. There are perhaps five or six lapses of time during the sequences, each one necessitating a change of costume, makeup, and position by the two characters. But the dialogue runs straight on without a break, from the first scene where Kane speaks lovingly to his wife, to the last where the wife silently picks up and is hidden behind a copy of the rival paper to Kane's.

Without seeing the picture again it is only possible to touch on what it has. In sound invention Welles seems inexhaustible. He varies it constantly and shatters at every turn the complacency of the critical hack, who never quite recovers from the effect of the first two or three minutes: the main title in silence, then the use of music with the death scene of Kane, then the sudden plunge into gaudy newsreel tempo as accompaniment to the "March of Time" film-within-a-film showing the legendary Kane's life in headlines. An essay or two could be written about the "March of Time" sequence alone. The scenes of Kane's earlier life are scratched as if the film were taken from newsreel archives, and a camera of early days has presumably been used, exposing fewer frames to the second than the cameras of today. The effect of the "real thing" is quite startling.

But the script, the approach to and treatment of the material, is a revolution in itself. It does everything that cannot, must not be done according to Hollywood's dreary "box-office" conventions. The story of a man's life begins with his death: he speaks a single word which all by itself gives every foot that follows pace and suspense. His story is unfolded through the efforts of a "March of Time" scout to discover the significance of this deathbed word: the strange word "Rosebud." You cannot possibly guess the answer, and the investigator never finds it, though Welles gives it to the audience in the final scene of all. The worst "crime" of the script—its most fascinating and praiseworthy feature—is that it not only darts about in time from Kane's boyhood to his old age, back to his heyday as a newspaper publisher, back again to his first day on his first paper, on again suddenly to his political and personal decay; not only that, but that it shows the same events several times over. But as each time they are seen through the eyes of a different person, the repetitions do more to build the whole structure of the character and his environment than new scenes could do. Here we are really in the cinema medium, in that and nothing else. What other mediums could show so forcefully that truth is not merely objective, but subjective also and at the same time? Not even the novel.

And what all this does is to make Kane the most three-dimensional human being who ever walked and talked on the screen—I would almost say the only one. Welles does not merely show us one aspect of the man and pound on it. He comes not to praise nor to indict Kane, but to reveal him, as he is and as others see him. The result is that profound pity is stirred up in the audience, and the indictment is not of a man but of environments and social and economic factors which make him what he becomes. The Hollywood axiom that men are born good or bad, and that wrongs and tragedies occur because Mr. Bad temporarily triumphs over Mr. Good, is shown up for the infantile and completely shopworn thing it is.

The implications of *Citizen Kane* for Hollywood and its future products can hardly be estimated at this time. A big man in the studios who was among those privileged to see *Kane* soon after it was finished, is said to have declared that not Hearst, but the top writers and sound men and cameramen and other experts had reason to be scared silly by what the picture revealed. He meant that *Kane* showed them all up as incompetents who need to go back to school to learn the first principles of the medium.

I do not share his concern for these people. Certainly, Hollywood has an extra-large quota of those phonies in high places who infest every sphere from politics to waterproof roofing. Anything in the way of showing them up and kicking them around that *Kane* can do will be a service to art and mankind. But by no means all of the craftsmen who have not been doing the things *Kane* does are "shown up" by *Kane*. The reason they have not done these things is not that they cannot do them but that they have not been allowed to do them.

Imagine, just for example, a regular Hollywood writer of even the most eminent class daring to submit to his producer a script like *Kane*'s! Imagine a makeup man daring to allow real sweat and agony to disorder the hair and face of the heroine as she comes out of a stupor after taking poison! Imagine a set designer putting the characters under real ceilings only a foot or two above their heads! Imagine a cameraman placing his lights so that almost half the time the faces are in shadow! Preposterous! Throw them out!

Yet does any film-goer really think that only Orson Welles and his staff are *capable* of such things? He need not think so. To say that there are in Hollywood a score of cameramen, a score of writers, a score of sound experts, a score of makeup artists—all equal to Orson's men in their own field—is probably to underestimate. For years they have been hoping and trying for a chance to show their skill and originality, but always the film salesman, speaking through the producer, has had the last word; and the film salesman is one trained in not seeing the wood for the trees. Those who are honest in Hollywood know that the regular craftsman, who earns his salary in studios year in and year out, is not allowed to show originality save within the tiny limits that the box-office tradition has laid down. Only when it is a best-selling novel does Hollywood make a *Grapes of Wrath*. And only an Orson Welles or a Chaplin, whose names cast a spell of magic even over the sales force and who are quite independent financially, can break the spells that bind the rank and file to formula. The slaves and houris of Hollywood are like the slaves and houris of Kane's empire, except that the chains of some of them are made of platinum. Yet when a Welles does come along and break the spell, and the box-office tune changes, the effect is like the big scene in *The Sleeping Beauty*. Suddenly tongues begin to talk, brains to operate, everything to move again.

It is just about certain that we shall now see another of Hollywood's copycat orgies, with whole films in which nobody's face is ever seen at all, time sequence is mixed up like a Christmas pudding, and every time lapse is shown by continuous dialogue over changing pictures of the same people. But with that, there will also be the release of a whole storehouse of original invention and craft skill which has been bottled up.

None of this is intended as any detraction from the stature of Orson Welles. Hollywood has no score, no dozen, of Welles'. Probably it has only one. He is bigger than any of them, or he could not have put *Citizen Kane* across. He would, I believe, be the first to admit that the things that seem miraculous in *Kane* could, taken individually, have been equalled by many other craftsmen in the departments concerned. But the unique quality he has is the ability to lead and to coordinate the skilled work of others. He does not try to tell the specialists on his staff how to play their own game, but recognizes the skill of each, and gives it full expression within a disciplined and ordered framework which can display it at its best. That, at least, is the impression *Kane* gives me. It is the work of many artists and yet, with and above that, the work of one, as great works of art in any medium have always been up to now. It is correctly described as "By Orson Welles"—not "produced" or "directed" or "from a story" by Welles, but *by* him. And because it is all *by* him, because of his conception and coordination of the work, his collaborators on camera and art direction and sound and all the rest shine more brightly.

He is the biggest man in Hollywood today. And he is the Prince Charming whose bold, smacking kiss on the brow of a bewitched art puts us all in his debt.

TANGYE LEAN

Citizen Kane tells a story, but it is impossible (I think) to notice all its implications and details at the first visit, and after another there is still information to be collected from other people. This fertility makes it a new kind of film, different, for instance, from the more obscure German films of the twenties, whose intricacy was just a question of plot. The details of *Citizen Kane* deepen and widen its revelation of character, and even when their logical point is overlooked, they still produce a certain effect, as lines of *Hamlet* which pass too quickly for the intelligence to recognize.

Technically it is perhaps a decade ahead of its contemporaries. For the first time, and with a touch of pride one can forgive, a film shows every room complete with its ceiling. Gone are the roofless thirties when the fantasy of Hollywood directors and the apartments they revealed had no limit but the sky. For the first time—and this is away from realism—"depth of focus" is so efficiently exploited that events in the background are as sharp as in medieval Flemish paintings. (The human eye cannot manage this completeness; in life we keep choosing between foreground, middle-distance, and background.) The camera is used originally, minimizing the number of cuts, while the microphone is allowed to pick up cross-currents of sound which predecessors have been at pains to smother. Realism is such that a cameraman—and I imagine almost no one else—notices the sun has shifted round two or three points on the face of a character while he relates a long section of the story. The technical strength of *Citizen Kane* is that it takes nothing for granted, no rule of thumb, no convention, least of all the convention that the nineties were glamorous, only one or two clichés.

From Horizon *4 (November 1941): 359–64.*

The plot seems complicated because we insist on reconstructing it in the orthodox time-sequence which Proust began to defy. Its outline in these terms is fairly simple. Born about 1866, died about now, Charlie Kane became one of our great irresponsible newspaper magnates. As a child an accident made him rich, and his mother insisted that he should be taken away from his games in the snow outside their Colorado shack for an education appropriate to his fortune. He hated leaving his sledge; he distrusted his mother's "You won't be lonely, Charles"; he raged, but was dragged away for good.

Twenty years later he entered journalism as a fighting Liberal, "the friend of the working man," whose motto was "all the news honestly," whether it was scandalous, profoundly shocking, or merely intimate. His circulations grew; his papers multiplied. He had a lust for controlling other people's opinions. He ran for Governor of New York State, but was defeated at the last moment by the exposure of his relations with a Miss Susan Alexander. That finished him politically. "You're not going to like organized labor one little bit, when you find it means your working man expects something as his right, and not your gift," his closest friend tells him. "Oh, boy, that's going to add up to something bigger than your privilege, and then I know what you'll do. Sail away to a desert island, probably, and lord it over the monkeys." (To which Kane, always smart, replies: "There'll probably be a few of them there to tell me when I do something wrong.")

Kane went to his desert island. But not yet, not till the sexual flop was as complete as the political flop. Because it wasn't yet certain that he had failed with women. There had been a lot, and he had quarrelled disastrously with his first wife, but Susan seemed more promising. The day after they married, he described her as a cross-section of the American public: but that was in her favor. As he had once championed the working man, so now he would transform her quavering soprano into the voice of a prima donna. What surprised him was that despite the headlines of two dozen newspapers and the erection of a $3,000,000 Opera House, he failed. Still more surprising was her desire to stop making herself ridiculous.

> KANE: You'll continue with your singing, Susan. I don't propose to have myself made ridiculous.
>
> SUSAN: *You* don't propose to have yourself made ridiculous! What about me? I'm the one that has to do the singing. I'm the one that gets the razzberries!

And Kane only desisted when she had all but successfully committed suicide. Then they went to Xanadu. He had built this castle with less taste than Kubla Khan but on an equally lavish site. Standing in 40,000

Florida acres, with subcastles in Baroque, Gothic, and Greek, it was surrounded by monkeys, elephants, and giraffes in cages. His art purchases rivalled those Napoleon accreted in the Louvre.

Susan: A person could go crazy in this dump. Nobody to talk to, nobody to have any fun with. Charlie, I want to go to New York. I wanta have fun. Please, Charlie . . . Charles, *please.* . . .

Kane: Our home is here, Susan. I don't care to visit New York.

He gave her parties with hundreds of guests. Cars processed along their private seaside, Negro bands played. She left him, and he died, muttering the odd word "Rosebud. . . ."

Simplified to this extent the story may seem like a suitable modern setting for George Arliss. On the screen it happens differently. It happens as a prodigious jumble of events torn out of their time sequence. First a three-minute impression of Xanadu with thick lips muttering "Rosebud . . ." and a hand relaxing on a glass ball which rolls down some steps and smashes. Then the life of Kane told as *March of Time* would tell it. Then the newsreel editors set out to discover the meaning of this word "Rosebud," and a long investigation goes on as if this was a puzzle for detectives. Five people who knew Kane well are interviewed, and in the course of these interviews, while time switches to and fro and the reels of the film are spent, we gradually get to know him. But no one knows anything about Rosebud; no one except at the end, Kane's butler, and he can only say that Kane muttered the word when his second wife deserted.

So the investigators, standing in the assembled bric-à-brac of Xanadu, give up the search. "If you put all this stuff together," says one of them, who has been toying with a jigsaw puzzle of Susan Kane's, "what would it spell?" "Rosebud?" suggests another. "I don't think so," the first replies. "I don't think any word can explain a man's life. No. I guess Rosebud is just a piece in a jigsaw puzzle, a missing piece."

But the camera sweeps up and back, revealing the full extent of the *objets d'art* which look from the distance exactly like a jigsaw puzzle, and then it dives purposefully down; over the Donatello Nativity and the fourth-century Venus, past the crates containing a Scottish castle, the urns, trays, gongs, screens, until it selects a single object which is being thrown into a furnace by workmen. It is the sledge called Rosebud from which Charlie Kane was forcibly separated in his childhood. And that, except for a little smoke, is the end.

Now I think this is a great film because you can leave it, as the investigators do, a minute before the end, and it remains an extraordinary comment on our old civilization and its values. For the first time someone in Hollywood is being serious, for instance, about journalism. "If the headline is big enough, it makes the news big enough," is one of Kane's principles, and this determination to adjust the facts to his desires extends to everything he touches, and applies particularly to his employees, who in return for high pay must be efficient writing-machines stripped of all principles of their own. It is true that the world does not wholly accept Kane—he is too much of a parody of its defects for that—but it marvels. "The greatest tycoon of this or any other century" is the view of the newsreel commentator, who places one of America's major financial scoundrels as the Grand Old Man of Wall Street. Kane is of course on speaking terms with the dictators and Prime Ministers of Europe, and false values are so firmly founded in him that rather than admit, even to himself, the true nature of these men and their world, he replies to a reporter, "I talked with the responsible leaders of the Great Powers—England, France, Germany, and Italy. They are too intelligent to embark upon a project which would mean the end of civilization as we know it. You can take my word for it, there will be no war."

False, false, false. . . . The criticism is hammered into us so effectively that *Citizen Kane* seems to have come from the studio of a post-war world rebuilding itself on a basis of new values. Hollywood has always accepted, if it did not go far to make, the early twentieth century; Orson Welles holds it up and says: "Look there, and there, and at that."

He is greatly helped by a cast devoid of "stars"; because of this and his one-man control as director and producer we get, instead of the familiar competition for a place in the arc-lights, an organic and unified picture.

If you leave a minute before the end, you see all this and more. But if you don't leave, and if you accept the discovery of "Rosebud" as something more significant than an O. Henry ending, a vast pattern of interrelated human themes becomes clear—as a different one does in the last volume of *A la Recherche du Temps Perdu*. We realize that when the child Charlie Kane was snatched away from his mother at her own instructions, a wound was inflicted on him that he didn't forget, that he spent his adult life trying to heal. He tried politically, fighting with crude and undiluted egotism for the rights of other people; he tried with women, and they resented his egotism even more bitterly than the workers did. He developed a megalomania whose roots lay in the situation he had been unable to control. "This Rosebud you're trying to find out about. . . ." says Kane's former manager. "Maybe that was something he lost. Mr. Kane was a man who lost almost everything he had." To which his closest friend adds "Love. . . . That's why he did everything. That's why he went into politics. It seems we weren't enough. He wanted all the voters to love him, too. All he wanted out of life was love. That's Charlie's story. How he lost it. You see he just didn't have any to give. Oh, he loved Charlie Kane, of course. Yeh. Very dearly. And his mother, I guess he always loved her."

His mother, but no one else. Is this what the twenties and thirties would have called Freud?

Technically, I have insisted, there are two very striking things about this film, the precise focus over the whole area of the screen and the overlapping of sounds so that two different sentences are often reaching our ears at the same time. We are forced by these devices to lay our own emphasis on the data, to make our own selection. Orson Welles even takes a perverse, sometimes slightly cheap, delight in heightening our difficulty. As an instance I would say that it is of the greatest possible relevance that Kane fell in love with Susan immediately after he had seen on her dressing table a crystal ball containing a snow-covered shack and a sledge. It is this crystal which reminds him of "Rosebud" when his wife leaves him, and which he holds when he dies. But the crystal has the same lack of prominence on the screen as Susan's hairbrushes, and most of the audience, if they noticed it, would probably not agree with me in thinking it of greater interest.

Orson Welles likes this confusion. He extends it beyond the technical management of light and sound. He will give us, partly because he is a first-class showman, five or ten superb minutes of chorus girls dancing as a background to a serious conversation, five minutes of a political speech by Kane, but only thirty seconds of the vital scene in which his mother sends him into exile. But Welles would certainly answer that life itself treats the important things in this arbitrary fashion. "A fellow will remember a lot of things you wouldn't think he'd remember," says Kane's manager when asked about Rosebud. "You take me. One day back in 1896 I was crossing over to Jersey on the ferry, and as we pulled out there was another ferry pulling in, and on it there was a girl waiting to get off. A white dress she had on. She was carrying a white parasol. I only saw her for one second. She didn't see me at all, but I'll bet a month hasn't gone by since that I haven't thought of that girl."

Equally, Orson Welles believes that the significant things that happen to us are the ones that get condensed, overlooked, forgotten. He does something to point the significance of the muddle, more than is done for us by life itself, but less than by a medical case history or a political novel. There is room, as in all good art, for you to take your choice. Freud would have been at liberty to pin Rosebud down as a symbol with the precise significance his experience had taught him to diagnose. Marx could have pointed to the necessary spiritual corruption involved in the possession of capital—"You know Mr. Bernstein, if I hadn't been very rich, I might have been a really great man." The perceptive agnostic can make what choice he likes within the limits of the material, but he feels an obligation to account for it more or less completely; the film has so obviously a meaning that he feels irritated if he cannot, or will not, see one that convinces him. It is worth noticing that some people are as outraged as their ancestors were by, say, *Hernani;* but this is not simply irritation at being confronted by a new art form, it is also a refusal to accept the implied criticisms of character and society.

Life is like this, and so is Proust's novel, but not up to now, Hollywood. Orson Welles is twenty-six, with say forty years of work ahead of him.

ESSAYS

"CITIZEN KANE Is Not about Louella Parsons' Boss"
by ORSON WELLES

In *Friday*'s coverage of *Citizen Kane* only two statements are strictly true. These are both too trivial to bear reprinting.

Among other things which aren't true, *Friday* says I've been in Hollywood two years, and that I've spent most of my time amusing myself. Actually, I've written four scripts, and the statistics concerning the average yearly output of producers, directors, script writers, and actors lucky enough to be in the A Division, show that however unsuccessful my efforts, I can't have had much time for recreation.

I've worked hard since I came to Hollywood—very hard on the shooting of *Kane* (normal hours 4 A.M. to 10 P.M.).

Friday says my "antic voyages ate into the night with a hundred overtime technicians hooraying for the fun." This means I haven't been doing my job for RKO, and if it were true, I should be fired. I can't help it if *Friday* doesn't take me seriously. I don't take myself seriously, but I'm very serious indeed about my work. Maybe it stinks, but I don't joke with other people's money.

In *Friday*'s article about *Citizen Kane* you have to look very closely to find the label "Sneak Preview." Anyway, it seems to me that "sneak preview" suggests that the picture involved is being reviewed, which ought to mean that the author of the article has seen the picture. *Friday*'s copy clearly indicates that nobody did.

Worst of all, *Friday* comments on Louella Parsons' lavish praise for me (in itself quite an overstatement of the facts) and puts these words into my mouth: "Wait until the woman finds out that the picture's about her boss." This is not a misquotation. *Friday*'s source invented it.

"Citizen Kane *Is Not about Louella Parsons' Boss" by Orson Welles,*
Friday 2 *(February 14, 1941): 9.*

Citizen Kane is not about Louella Parsons' boss. It is the portrait of a fictional newspaper tycoon, and I have never said or implied to anyone that it is anything else.

Citizen Kane is the story of a search by a man named Thompson, the editor of a news digest (similar to the *March of Time*), for the meaning of Kane's dying words. He hopes they'll give the short the angle it needs. He decides that a man's dying words ought to explain his life. Maybe they do. He never discovers what Kane's mean, but the audience does. His researches take him to five people who know Kane well—people who liked him or loved him or hated his guts. They tell five different stories, each biased, so that the truth about Kane, like the truth about any man, can only be calculated, by the sum of everything that has been said about him.

Kane, we are told, loved only his mother—only his newspaper—only his second wife—only himself. Maybe he loved all of these, or none. It is for the audience to judge. Kane was selfish and selfless, an idealist, a scoundrel, a very big man and a very little one. It depends on who's talking about him. He is never judged with the objectivity of an author, and the point of the picture is not so much the solution of the problem as its presentation. The easiest way to draw parallels between Kane and other famous publishers is not to see the picture.

Citizen Kane is the portrait of a public man's private life. I have met some publishers, but I know none of them well enough to make them possible as models.

Friday ran a series of stills from *Kane,* whose captions were inaccurate descriptions of the action of the picture. Constant reference was made to the career of William Randolph Hearst. This is unfair to Hearst and to *Kane.*

Retractions are notoriously valueless, but *Citizen Kane*'s producer is nonetheless grateful to *Friday* for this chance to keep the record straight.

Score for a Film
by BERNARD HERRMANN

Citizen Kane was the first motion picture on which I had ever worked. I had heard of the many handicaps that exist for a composer in Hollywood. One was the great speed with which scores often had to be written—sometimes in as little as two or three weeks. Another was that the composer seldom had time to do his own orchestration. And again—that once the music was written and conducted, the composer had little to say about the sound levels or dynamics of the score in the finished film.

Not one of these conditions prevailed during the production of *Citizen Kane*.

I was given twelve weeks in which to do my job. This not only gave me ample time to think about the film and to work out a general artistic plan for the score, but also enabled me to do my own orchestration and conducting.

I worked on the film, reel by reel, as it was being shot and cut. In this way I had a sense of the picture being built, and of my own music being a part of that building. Most musical scores in Hollywood are written after the film is entirely finished, and the composer must adapt his music to the scenes on the screen. In many scenes in *Citizen Kane* an entirely different method was used, many of the sequences being tailored to match the music.

This was particularly true in the numerous photographic "montages," which are used throughout the film to denote the passing of time. When I first saw the picture I felt that it might be interesting to write complete musical numbers for these montages. In other words, instead of a mere atmospheric or rhythmic cue, a brief piece would be

---

"Score for a Film" by Bernard Herrmann. From The New York Times *(May 25, 1941)*. Copyright © *1941 by* The New York Times Company. Reprinted by permission of The New York Times.

written. Welles agreed, and once the music was set, cut many of his sequences to match the length of the pieces.

The most striking illustration of this method may be found in the "breakfast montage" between Kane and his first wife. Here, in the space of three of four minutes, Welles shows the rise and fall of affection between two married people. The setting is a breakfast table. The young couple enters, gay and very much in love. They talk for a few seconds, then the scene changes. Once more we see them at the breakfast table, but the atmosphere has changed. Discord is beginning to creep into the conversation. Brief scene after brief scene follows, each showing the gradual breakdown of their affection, until finally they read their newspapers, opposite each other, in silence.

For this montage, I used the old classic form of the theme and variations. A waltz in the style of Waldteufel is the theme. It is heard during the first scene. Then, as discord crops up, the variations begin. Each scene is a separate variation. Finally, the waltz theme is heard bleakly played in the high registers of the violins.

Earlier in the film the scenes in the office showing Kane's newspaper activities are treated in a similar way. This part of the picture takes place in the eighteen-nineties, and, to match its mood, I used the various dance forms popular at that time. Thus, the montage showing the increase of circulation of *The Inquirer* is done as a can-can scherzo. *The Inquirer*'s campaign against the traction trust is done in the form of a gallop. Kane and his friend Leland arrive at the office to the rhythm of early ragtime. This whole section, in itself, contains a kind of ballet suite in miniature.

Leitmotivs are used in *Citizen Kane* to give unity to the score as a whole. I am not a great believer in the "leitmotiv" as a device for motion picture music—but in this film its use was practically imperative, because of the story itself and the manner in which it is unfolded.

There are two main motifs. One—a simple four-note figure in the brass—is that of Kane's power. It is given out in the very first two bars of the film. The second motif is that of Rosebud. Heard as a solo on the vibraphone, it first appears during the death scene at the very beginning of the picture. It is heard again and again throughout the film under various guises, and if followed closely, is a clue to the ultimate identity of Rosebud itself.

The motif of power is also transformed, becoming a vigorous piece of ragtime, a hornpipe polka, and at the end of the picture, a final commentary on Kane's life.

In handling these motifs I used a great deal of what might be termed "radio scoring." The movies frequently overlook opportunities for musical clues which last only a few seconds—that is, from five to fifteen seconds at the most—the reason being that the eye usually covers the transition. On the other hand, in radio drama, every scene must be bridged by some sort of sound device, so that even five seconds of music becomes a vital instrument in telling the ear that the scene is shifting. I felt that in this film, where the photographic contrasts were often so sharp and sudden, a brief cue—even two or three chords—might heighten the effect immeasurably. In addition to all this psychological and structural music, *Citizen Kane* is full of incidental music of all kinds. There is a large section of news-reel music, bands and hurdy-gurdy tunes, there is even an opera recitative and aria. All of these are realistic music. The news-reel music during the "News on the March" sequence was selected from the RKO files, and used in typical news-reel manner. The opera aria, "Salammbo," was composed in the style of the nineteenth-century French Oriental operatic school.

In orchestrating the picture I avoided, as much as possible, the realistic sound of a large symphony orchestra. The motion picture sound-track is an exquisitely sensitive medium, and with skillful engineering a simple bass flute solo, the pulsing of a bass drum, or the sound of muted horns can often be far more effective than half a hundred musicians playing away. Save for the opera sequence, some of the ballet montages, and a portion of the final scene, most of the cues were orchestrated for unorthodox instrumental combinations.

Sound effects were blended many times in *Citizen Kane,* with the music, to add intensity to certain scenes. This also was a carry-over from radio technique. The best example of this may be found in the "suicide" montage, which portrays the chaos of the second Mrs. Kane's operatic career. Here, sound-tracks of her voice were blended with a rhythmical musical motif to produce an effect of mounting hysteria.

Music also was used in place of an actual sound-effect, as in the jig-saw puzzle scenes at Xanadu, where it simulates the endless ticking of a clock.

Finally, a word about the "dubbing" of the music—that is, the recording of the score into the final sound-track. Too often, in Hollywood, the composer has little to say about this technical procedure, and the result is that some of the best film music is often submerged to scarcely audible levels. Welles and I felt that music which was intended only as atmospheric background should be originally written for that purpose, and not toned down in the dubbing room. In other words, the dynamics of all music in the picture should be planned ahead of time so that the final dubbing is merely a transference process.

With this in mind two full weeks were spent in the dubbing room, and music under our supervision was often re-recorded six or seven times before the proper dynamic level was achieved. The result is an exact projection of the original ideas in the score. Technically, no composer could ask for more.

How I Broke the Rules in CITIZEN KANE
by GREGG TOLAND, A. S. C.

There's been a good deal of gratifying discussion recently about the photography of Orson Welles's first movie, *Citizen Kane*. The gist of the talk has been that the cinematography in that film was "daring" and "advanced," and that I violated all the photographic commandments and conventions in shooting the picture.

Right away I want to make a distinction between "commandment" and "convention." Photographically speaking, I understand a commandment to be a rule, axiom, or principle, an incontrovertible fact of photographic procedure which is unchangeable for physical and chemical reasons. On the other hand, a convention, to me, is a usage which has become acceptable through repetition. It is a tradition rather than a rule. With time the convention becomes a commandment, through force of habit. I feel that the limiting effect is both obvious and unfortunate.

With these definitions in mind, I'll admit that I defied a good many conventions in filming *Citizen Kane*. Orson Welles was insistent that the story be told most effectively, letting the Hollywood conventions of movie-making go hang if need be. With such whole-hearted backing I was able to test and prove several ideas generally accepted as being radical in Hollywood circles.

Welles's use of the cinematographer as a real aid to him in telling the story, and his appreciation of the camera's story-telling potentialities helped me immeasurably. He was willing—and this is very rare in Hollywood—that I take weeks to achieve a desired photographic effect.

The photographic approach to *Citizen Kane* was planned and con-

"*How I Broke the Rules in* Citizen Kane" *by Gregg Toland. From* Popular Photography Magazine *8 (June 1941): 55. Reprinted by permission of* Popular Photography Magazine.

sidered long before the first camera turned. That is also unconventional in Hollywood, where most cinematographers learn of their next assignments only a few days before the scheduled shooting starts. Altogether, I was on the job for a half year, including preparation and actual shooting.

Although it was Welles's first effort in movies, he came to the job with a rare vision and understanding of camera purpose and direction. It was his idea that the technique of filming should never be evident to the audience. He wanted to avoid the established Hollywood conventions, most of which are accepted by audiences because of their frequent use. And this frequent use of conventions is dictated by pressure of time and reluctance to deviate from the accepted.

As a case in point, depth of field nearly always is sacrificed in Hollywood productions. The normal human eye sees everything before it (within reasonable distance) clearly and sharply. There is no special or single center of visual sharpness in real life. But the Hollywood cameras focus on a center of interest, and allow the other components of a scene to "fuzz out" in those regions before and beyond the focal point.

The attainment of an approximate human-eye focus was one of our fundamental aims in *Citizen Kane*. It took a great deal of doing, but we proved that it can be done.

We solved the depth-of-field problem by means of preproduction testing and experiment. We built our system of "visual reality" on the well-known fact that lenses of shorter focal length are characterized by comparatively greater depth, and that stopping down a lens increases the depth even further.

The tendency in Hollywood has been to stop down to $f3.5$ occasionally in filming interiors. More often the working aperture is between $f2.3$ and $f3.2$. The use of the $f3.5$ aperture is still uncommon enough to be cause for conversation in the film capital. Yet any professional or amateur who has used short-focus lenses knows that the increase in depth obtained by stopping down from $f2.3$ to $f3.5$ can make quite a difference.

But we wanted to stop down considerably further. By experimenting with high-speed films we discovered that lens aperture could be reduced appreciably, but that we still weren't able to stop down enough for our purposes. This meant that an increased illumination level had to be obtained. And since we were already violating Hollywood tradition by using ceilinged sets, we were unable to step up illumination by means of extra lights mounted on catwalks or strung above the scene.

The Vard "Opticoating" system developed at the California Institute of Technology, proved to be one factor in the eventual solution of our lighting problem. Being essentially a method of treating lens surfaces, Opticoating eliminates refraction, permits light to penetrate instead of scattering, and thus increases lens speed by as much as a full stop. Our coated lenses also permitted us to shoot directly into lights without anything like the dire results usually encountered.

Another aid in solving our small-aperture problem was the twin-arc broadside lamp, developed for Technicolor work. We began to employ these lamps before we hit upon the use of the high-speed film which we eventually chose. The combination of coated lenses, arc broadside lamps, and the fastest available film made it possible to photograph nearly all interior scenes at an aperture of $f8$ or even smaller. I shot several scenes at $f11$ and $f16$. That's a big jump from $f2.3$ and it's certainly unconventional in Hollywood filming.

Even the standard 47- and 50-mm. lenses afford great depth of field when stopped down to $f11$ or $f16$. And the shorter-focus wide-angle lenses act virtually like human eyes, providing almost universal focus at such small apertures. In some cases we were able to hold sharp focus over a depth of 200 feet.

I referred previously to the unconventional use of ceilinged sets. The *Citizen Kane* sets have ceilings because we wanted reality, and we felt that it would be easier to believe a room was a room if its ceiling could be seen in the picture. Furthermore, lighting effects in unceilinged rooms generally are not realistic because the illumination comes from unnatural angles.

We planned most of our camera setups to take advantage of the ceilings, in some cases even building the sets so as to permit shooting upward from floor level. None of the sets was rigged for overhead lighting, although occasionally necessary backlighting was arranged by lifting a small section of the ceiling and using a light through the opening. The deep sets called for unusually penetrating lamps, and the twin-arc broadsides mentioned earlier filled the bill. The ceilings gave us another advantage in addition to realism—freedom from worry about microphone shadow, the bugaboo of all sound filming. We were able to place our mikes above the muslin ceiling, which allowed them to pick up sound but not to throw shadows.

There were other violations of Hollywood tradition in the photographic details of *Citizen Kane*. One of them resulted from Welles's insistence that scenes should flow together smoothly and imperceptibly. Accordingly, before actual shooting began, everything had been planned with full realization of what the camera could bring to the audience. We arranged our action so as to avoid direct cuts, to permit panning or dollying from one angle to another whenever that type of camera action fitted the continuity. By way of example, scenes which conventionally would require a shift from closeup to full shot were planned so that the action would take place simultaneously in extreme foreground and extreme background.

Our constant efforts toward increasing realism and making mechanical details imperceptible led eventually to the solution of all the problems we had created for ourselves. As we avoided direct cuts, so we steered clear of traditional transitions. Most of the transitions in *Citizen Kane* are lap-dissolves in which the background dissolves from one scene to the next shortly before the players in the foreground are dissolved. This was accomplished rather simply with two light-dimming outfits, one for the actors and one for the set.

The dissolve is begun by dimming the lights on the background, eventually fading it out entirely. Then the lights on the people are dimmed to produce a fade-out on them. The fade-in is made the same way, fading in the set lights first, then the lights for the people.

Intercutting was eliminated wherever possible, with the idea of achieving further visual simplification. Instead of following the usual practice of cutting from a close-up to an "insert" (which explains or elaborates upon the close-up), we made a single, straight shot, compressing the whole scene into a single composition.

Here's an example. Where the idea is to show an actor reading something, we don't show a close-up of the actor and then follow it with a cut to the reading matter "insert." We simply compose the shot with the actor's head on one side of the frame and the reading matter on the other. In one such case in the filming of *Citizen Kane* the actor's head was less than sixteen inches from the lens, the reading matter was about three feet away, and a group of men in the background was twelve to eighteen feet away. Yet all three components of this scene—actor in foreground, reading matter, and group—are sharp and clear to the audience.

My focusing was based on the principle of depth of field. Knowing the focal length and other characteristics of the lenses we were using, I worked out the various focal points as I came to them. By following a depth-of-field table in using any lens, you can always tell just where to set your focus in order to attain overall sharpness within required limits. It's an important fact, however, that much depends upon the properties of the lens in use at the time—and its characteristics should be determined carefully before any attempt is made to use this zone-focusing technique.

Such differences as exist between the cinematography in *Citizen Kane* and the camera work on the average Hollywood product are based on the rare opportunity provided me by Orson Welles, who was in complete sympathy with my theory that the photography should fit the story. I have been trying to follow that principle for some time in an effort to provide visual variety as well as a proper photographic vehicle for the plot. Fitting *Wuthering Heights* and *Grapes of Wrath* and *Long Voyage Home* to an identical photographic pattern would be unfair to director, writer, actors, and audience.

Style too often becomes deadly sameness. In my opinion, the day of highly stylized cinematography is passing, and is being superseded by a candid, realistic technique and an individual approach to each new film subject.

You will accomplish much more by fitting your photography to the story instead of limiting the story to the narrow confines of conventional photographic practice. And as you do so you'll learn that the movie camera is a flexible instrument, with many of its possibilities still unexplored. New realms remain to be discovered by amateurs and professionals who are willing to think about it and take the necessary time to make the thought a reality.

CITIZEN KANE:
Background and a Critique
by ROY A. FOWLER

MORE TROUBLE

It seemed that Orson Welles had now fully explored the world of drama; he had had as big a success as it seemed likely he would ever have; he had had as great a failure as even his enemies would wish him to have. There remained one popular medium of art to which he had not yet turned his mind—or if not his mind, his hand. It was, of course, the film. To many (perhaps only the cynical) it was certain that sooner or later, too, Hollywood would attempt to sujugate this fresh, new, essentially showmanlike personality. Notwithstanding later events, Welles was lucky that he went to Hollywood for RKO Radio. This firm, in process of extensive reorganization, was headed by George J. Schaefer and it was he, at that time the most enlightened and progressive man to be head of a major Hollywood studio, who offered Welles a contract.

The man who had been suggested by *Life* as the successor to Max Reinhardt was, however, not interested in proposals that would involve any inferiority of status on his part. If he were to make films, he wanted the greatest possible freedom—and on those terms he was awarded his contract. In the first week of August, 1939, Orson Welles was signed by RKO Radio Pictures, Inc., to make one picture a year in which, at his own volition, he could be producer, director, writer, or actor. His remuneration would be 25 percent of the gross profits of each film, on which he received an advance of $150,000. The trade papers of that week carried a several-page advertisement of future RKO

"Citizen Kane: Background and a Critique" [editor's title]. From *Orson Welles: A First Biography* (*London: Pendulum, 1946*). Reprinted by permission of the author.

product at the end of which was the tiny legend: "Just Signed! . . . Orson Welles. . . . Spectacular genius of the Show World—brilliant actor and director, to make one picture a year. . . . and *what* a picture is planned for his first." There were, as a matter of fact, several pictures planned as his first before one materialized, but all that this involved was in the future months—which were to be quite unpleasant for Welles. Unaware of his pending tribulations, however, Orson Welles with John Houseman, Herbert Drake, and other members of the Mercury group, flew to Hollywood in those early weeks of August. Welles had a beard and a contract: general opinion was that he had done it again.

Three Thousand Miles Away and Still More Trouble

It was both the beard and the contract that did it. Nobody liked the beard, everybody hated the contract. Like peeved little children, the population of Hollywood indulged in nose-thumbing at the errant genius newly arrived in their midst. The beard, a particularly lush one, had been grown in anticipation of the part he would play in his first film—an adaptation of Joseph Conrad's novel, *Heart of Darkness*.

On being shown around the RKO Pathé lot at Culver City, the studios at which he was to commence filming, Welles remarked, "This is the biggest electric train a boy ever had!" His attitude thus seemed, to those who had lived in Hollywood for many years and who stood no chance whatsoever of obtaining a contract such as his, to be that of a little boy on a new kind of outing or with a new Xmas present. It is understandable that they were bitter: it was natural, therefore, that everybody should band together to laugh, jeer, sneer, and spit at him. His first party, to which all the prominent members of the movie colony were invited, was ignored and boycotted. Because of his beard he was sent, firstly, a bearded ham and then, later, by a Beverly Hills firm of interior decorators who somewhat surpassed themselves, a black crocheted chenille snood replete with a fringe containing mothballs. His tie was deliberately severed by an attacker in a public restaurant; some attempted to insert full-page advertisements in the trade papers ordering him out of Hollywood. Gene Lockhart, the actor and writer, obliged with a piece of doggerel that many found amusing:

> Little Orson Annie's come to our house to play,
> An' josh the motion pitchurs up and skeer the stars away,
> An' shoo the Laughtons off the lot an' build the sets an' sweep
> An' wind the film an' write the talk an' earn her board-an'-keep;
> An' all of us other acters, when our pitchur work is done,

We set around the Derby bar an' has the mostest fun,
A-listenin' to the me-tales 'at Annie tells about,
An' the Gobblewelles 'll git YOU
Ef you DON'T WATCH OUT!

Although, ostensibly, paying little attention to these happenings, Welles was hurt. There were, of course, faults on both sides although it is doubtful if his merited the treatment he received; he has always felt that. "When I came to Hollywood," he said recently, "I was treated badly. I'm just now beginning to get over it. Now, I'm less hot-headed."

The studio saw little of him during those first few weeks. He was enthroned in a six-hundred-dollar-a-month mansion atop a Brentwood Hill where, surrounded by Houseman, Drake (his publicity agent and formerly of the N.Y. *Herald-Tribune*), and countless secretaries, he prepared *Heart of Darkness*. "It's an adventure drama, localed in Darkest Africa," he said. "I'll be the central character in the picture. We're doing a lot of rewriting."

As his first effort in motion-picture writing, Welles's script of this novel is an amazing achievement. The story is, roughly, of a man called Marlow's trip up a jungle river on a ramshackle steamboat to meet and rescue a fabulous character named Kurtz. In the script it is the camera that plays Marlow's part: it sees everything with Marlow's eyes; people talk to it and it to them, yet it is never seen. Thus, for the first time in a major film was an attempt to be made to parallel the "I" form of narrative writing—Conrad's novel is written in the first person singular. Welles had grown the exciting beard preparatory to playing Kurtz.

Heart of Darkness was due to roll on October 10, 1939. It had a high budget which started at $500,000 and grew to $1,100,000. With the outbreak of war in Europe, and the consequent loss of many markets, RKO wanted to cut down the budget considerably. Dita Parlo, whom Welles wanted as the feminine lead was, because an Austrian, interned in France as an enemy alien. The starting date was postponed until October 31. Many heads happily nodded in Hollywood. In the third week of October, the erstwhile director started to rehearse his cast for the film. RKO however, gradually regretting their impetuosity, were by now definitely against making the film, which they considered too experimental. They had a second subject lined up for him—an English thriller by Nicholas Blake (Cecil Day Lewis), *The Smiler with a Knife* —which they suggested as an alternative. Welles, more interested in his first script, promised to make this second picture for nothing if he were allowed to do the Conrad. RKO agreed and everything seemed happily settled.

The production department came through with the next difficulty. The extensive miniature set required for *Heart of Darkness* would take a considerable time to prepare and so, in late December, it was decided that *The Smiler with a Knife* would become the first production on the schedule. This, however, had a feminine character as the largest part. RKO maintained that a popular star with acting ability was essential for the rôle, and suggested Carole Lombard or Rosalind Russell. These turned it down completely, however, since Welles's script was very unorthodox and they were apprehensive about their fate at the hands of the novice director that Welles was.

So this film, too, was indefinitely postponed and Welles went to work upon the third subject on his schedule, *Citizen Kane*: in collaboration with Herman J. Mankiewicz, he had this script ready by July, 1940. In the months that he had been in Hollywood, Welles had run over in the studio's projection rooms much of the most significant footage ever shot. Afterwards, he took his unit into a sound-stage and spent many weeks learning the practical nature of lights, cameras, cranes, microphones. He learned what could be done with them and disbelieved what could not. He did profess himself, at one point, completely mystified as to the duties and function of a "producer," but this did not materially affect his plans.

At last, exactly a year after he had flown to Hollywood, a year during which many knowing and smug smiles had been smiled, Orson Welles took the floor with *Citizen Kane*. The date was July 30, 1940. To prove they had really allowed him to start, RKO invited the Hollywood press to see him at work. Some, apparently, were duly impressed, since the *Motion Picture Herald* for that week carried a paragraph heading: "Silence! Genius at work."

They were right, too.

After fifteen weeks on the floor, during which the Wellesian legend in Hollywood grew and grew and grew, *Citizen Kane* went to the cutting rooms on October 23, 1940. Cutting, dubbing, scoring, and model work occupied the next few weeks, after which, in the first days of January 1941, the studio had its first show copy of the film ready. The movie colony sat back gleefully, waiting for the balloon to burst.

Now begins a fabulous history.

Mr. William Randolph Hearst, colorful and famous newspaper baron of the USA, had as his papers' Hollywood representative Miss Louella Parsons. It was she who had been, for the past eighteen months, one of Welles's supporters. Not so very many months before this January 1941, before *Kane* had gone on the floor, Miss Parsons and a few others had begun to jeer at RKO for Welles's long, inactive sojourn on their lot.

The film finished, however, Miss Parsons began to hear queer stories and strange rumors. They were reported back to her employer who was both interested and annoyed: investigations were ordered. The second week in January, Miss Parsons and two Hearst lawyers saw the film at the RKO studio. She telegraphed her chief that the film was, in part, an unauthorized biography of William Randolph Hearst and such a one that showed him in an unfavorable light. Mr. Hearst immediately requested that the film be withheld from circulation.

A Thousand and One Nights

George Schaefer, RKO's president, heard Mr. Hearst's summons and politely disobeyed. He remarked they were giving "no serious consideration" to Hearst's proposal and set a release date of February 14. They were preparing, he said, an advertising campaign that would be "one of the most far-reaching ever launched for an attraction by RKO Radio Pictures." The preliminary advertisements alone were intended to reach fifty million American readers.

This first counter now had a few interesting repercussions. Herman Mankiewicz had, earlier in the year, lodged a protest with the Screen Writers' Guild demanding full screen credit for his work on the picture. When suddenly the battle of words and wits between RKO, Welles, and Hearst broke out, he forthwith lost all interest and his protest to the Guild was withdrawn. With the strange mind that "front offices" reputedly have, the studio, at the end of January, decided to give him the credit he no longer wanted.

Another person also entered the field. It was Miss Hedda Hopper, columnist and actress, who remarked that "Mr. Hearst got wind of it and his reviewer finally got around to seeing it. Then the fat was in the fire. . . ." It has been suggested that this battle over the release of *Kane* was a bout to decide to whom Hollywood belonged—to Miss Hopper or to Miss Parsons. The affair may, in its middle period, have developed into that but it was not, most certainly, in it that it had its origins. Miss Hopper, riding in the cause of Welles, announced she would broadcast a history of his life in six episodes, starting February 3. Although such a short time had elapsed since its commencement, *l'affaire Kane* was Hollywood property, with most of the industry's top executives on the side of nonrelease. It was an affair to be settled entirely outside the industry's trade organizations for it in no way concerned them. The Hays office could not intervene since, upon perusal of the script the previous July, they had discovered no transgression of the Production Code.[1] However, it was said that both Sam Goldwyn and Louis B. Mayer, executive producer of Metro-Goldwyn-Mayer, had

[1] [See this volume, p. 145, for a letter from the Production Code Office.]

telephoned Miss Hopper, using extreme pressure, begging her to cancel her radio biography. They felt the industry could not afford to be the target for such a concerted attack as was promised from the Hearst papers and that, as well, Mr. Hearst had always been a very good friend of the industry—particularly some sections of it. Miss Hopper, a personal friend of Welles, informed him of these actions and forthwith took to the air with her broadcast, on the appointed date. Miss Parsons, meanwhile, was reported to have contacted David Sarnoff (president of RCA, a company controlling RKO, chairman of NBC and a former chairman of the RKO board), Joseph Schenck of 20th-Century-Fox, Nicholas Schenck of MGM, Van Schmus, and the Rockefellers in her attempt to have the film withdrawn. There was also beginning to be much talk at this time of a pool being formed by Hollywood to buy and destroy the negative of the picture. Welles, of course, was violently against this. In Detroit, Hearst's *Times,* which had been publicizing its projected serialization of the novel *Kitty Foyle,* then in release as an RKO film, stopped its blurb and nothing was heard more of *Kitty Foyle* therein.

On January 27, at an Author's Club luncheon in Los Angeles, immediately prior to flying to New York, Welles, with Puckish impudence, flung further fuel onto the fire by declaring, "When I get *Citizen Kane* off my mind, I'm going to work on an idea for a great picture based on the life of William Randolph Hearst." In New York, it was indignantly denied that the film was to be shown to the "Sage of San Simeon" and that, then, any cuts he desired would be made. RKO's and Welles's standpoint was that there was nothing in the film connected in any way with Hearst save that his name was mentioned as a living person, contemporary to Kane. It was generally agreed in legal circles that Hearst's grounds for a court action were practically non-existent.

On January 26, an extension had been signed to Welles's contract with RKO. He was still to make three pictures (of which the first was *Kane*) but was to have more time in which to do them. Welles was, now, in New York, preparing his first legitimate production in two years. Gregg Toland, his cameraman on *Kane,* was in Mexico on a holiday-cum-location trip: the second Welles film was to be made in Mexico and had to be started before April 1st. Welles was to make this film for nothing since, although he had never made *Heart of Darkness,* he was still under contract to make "Production No. 2" free. Welles's script for this picture, to be photographed in Mexico City and on the Mexican welt, was partly original and partly based on Arthur Calder Marshall's novel *The Way to Santiago*: it was certain that Dolores del Rio, Welles's then fiancée, would star. The ban in the Hearst papers on reviewing, mentioning, or advertising all RKO pictures was lifted on January 31st. It had lasted only a week in most places, two weeks in others. In various cities, however, Hearst papers desultorily continued the childish practice.

At this time the film represented, in RKO money, $786,000, of which $746,000 represented actual production costs and $40,000 the money so far expended in advertising the property. As well as this, RKO had advanced $150,000 to Welles as his expectancy on the picture's gross. Most of this latter sum had gone to the Mercury to pay off the heavy debts incurred when *Five Kings* had failed two years before. RKO were therefore interested in releasing the film to amortize their money invested in it, while Welles was merely determined to have the film shown in order to answer his Hollywood critics. This $150,000 was all he had received from RKO: he had paid his expenses with salary from radio work and from a couple of lecture tours. The Mercury Players' wages on the film had been included in the film's production cost. Welles's plans were now to finish his current Broadway play, *Native Son*, return to Hollywood where he would quickly make the two pictures for which he was contracted, and then return to Broadway in the winter to play Lear. He hoped to take *King Lear* after an eight to ten weeks' run, on tour, after which he would return to Hollywood in the summer of 1942 for more film work.

He had by his contract, it was now announced, a legal right to insist that *Kane* be released, or failing that to buy it back from RKO. Since he and George Schaefer were friends, however, many considered it unlikely that he would take the matter to court. The controversy had, by this time, caused a split in the RKO board. Schaefer and others were in favor of the release of *Kane*: the other faction was just as violently against it. So long as there was a difference of opinion, the film could not be released.

In the week of February 16, the Hearst press manufactured almost out of nothing a *deus ex machina* with which to give Hollywood a foretaste of things to come should not the master's word be obeyed. In that week there came before the courts an action brought by Monsieur Joseph N. Ermolieff against RKO Radio Pictures and George Schaefer. The plaintiff, a refugee European producer, sued the company for an alleged "breach of contract" with the nonproduction of his play, purchased by RKO: he demanded $1,047,000 in damages and was awarded $7,000. Schaefer had been named as a codefendant with RKO but was eliminated from the action by the court. Notwithstanding, from coast to coast next day every Hearst paper headlined the story, insisting that Schaefer had been named codefendant. Every one of Hearst's seventeen dailies carried headlines similar to that of the Milwaukee *Sentinel*, which proclaimed: "CHARGES THAT RKO

Orson Welles, about 1940.

Young Kane, his parents, Thatcher, and "Rosebud."

Kane, Bernstein, and Leland: "A Declaration of Principles."

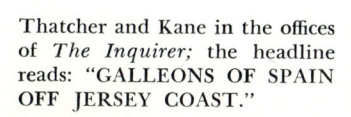

Thatcher and Kane in the offices of *The Inquirer;* the headline reads: "GALLEONS OF SPAIN OFF JERSEY COAST."

Kane and Emily at breakfast at the end of the famous marriage disintegration sequence.

Kane campaigning for governor.

Kane, Emily, Susan, and Gettys at Susan's apartment.

Kane threatening to send Gettys to Sing Sing.

Kane and Susan at Xanadu.

BROKE CONTRACT!" The Los Angeles *Herald-Examiner* carried its story under a seven-column headline.[2]

The following Sunday's New York *Mirror* (also owned by Hearst) carried a violent attack by Lee Mortimer, its film critic, written presumably on orders from above, on Hollywood in general and RKO in particular.

The controversy was now public property in the big towns and the RKO exchanges were deluged with enquiries about the film. Two days before the date set for its release, February 14, no dates for showings had been taken by these exchanges. The head office circulated them that the film might be road-shown. In *Variety,* March 11, Schaefer said: "A free speech, a free press, and a screen free for expression tell the story of American democracy. They merit no criticism. They need no defense."

Then, suddenly, RKO set press previews for March 12: everything was ready for them. Lists of names had been drawn up, telegrams of invitation were written out. Only Schaefer's word was needed in order to go ahead. It should have been given on March 10, but was not forthcoming. Now, even the Mercury was split. There were those who still thought, with Welles, that Schaefer would release the film: the others were convinced he was merely "stalling." With the latest move a final deciding blow, Welles called newspapermen together at his apartment in the Ambassador Hotel, New York, and announced that in his own name and in that of the Mercury Theatre he would file suit against RKO for breach of contract. The film should have been released, he said, within three months of the date of delivery—and RKO were now even disputing this. His statement read:

> I believe that the public is entitled to see *Citizen Kane.* For me to stand by while this picture was being suppressed would constitute a breach of faith with the public on my part as a producer. I have at this moment sufficient financial backing to buy *Citizen Kane* from RKO and to release it myself. Under my contract with RKO, I have the right to demand that the picture be released and to bring legal action to force its release. RKO must release *Citizen Kane.* If it does not do so immediately, I have instructed my attorney to commence proceedings. I have been advised that strong pressure is being brought to bear in certain quarters to cause the withdrawal of my picture *Citizen Kane* because of an alleged resemblance between incidents in the picture and incidents in the life of Mr. William

---

[2] "If the headline is big enough, it makes the news big enough."—A line spoken by Charles Foster Kane in the film *Citizen Kane.*

Randolph Hearst. Any such attempts at suppression would involve a serious interference with freedom of speech and with the integrity of the moving-picture industry as the foremost medium of artistic expression in the country. There is nothing in the facts to warrant the situation that has arisen. *Citizen Kane* was not intended to have nor has it any reference whatsoever to Mr. Hearst or to any other living person. No statement to the contrary has ever been authorized by me. *Citizen Kane* is the story of a wholly fictitious character. The script for *Citizen Kane* was scrutinized and approved by both RKO Radio Pictures and the Hays Office. No one in these organizations nor anyone associated with me in the production of the picture believed that it represented anything but the psychological analysis of an imaginary individual. I regret exceedingly that anyone should interpret *Citizen Kane* to have a bearing upon any living person or should impugn the artistic purposes of its producers.

Herbert Drake, Welles's publicity agent, remarked that Welles would show it "in tents" if need be and that, should he buy it, he would "probably open it at Soldiers' Field on four screens and saw Dolores in half at each intermission."

At the same press conference, when asked about this second film, Welles said: "I'll be glad to go ahead with the picture if it is satisfactory to the company." This was the film to be made without pay and Welles denied that he had refused to make it under these conditions or that RKO had agreed to pay him anything. Schaefer is reported to have telephoned him from Hollywood that week and have asked him not to "do anything legal until I arrive." He would, he said, take it up with the board of directors once more when he arrived in New York. Floyd B. Odlum, head of the Atlas Corporation, with it a large holder of RKO stock and also reputed controller of the vast Hearst empire, was variously reported to be leaving everything to Schaefer or to be cogitating the final decision. It was presumably at the board meeting to which Schaefer referred that this final decision was taken, although nothing was made public for several more weeks.

Reputedly, hundreds of people had now seen *Citizen Kane* at private showings. Among them was Henry Luce who, with his *Time* and *Life* cohorts, gave the film very good reviews in his two main magazines. It was denied that Luce, never a great friend of Hearst, was one of those backing Welles in his attempt to buy back the film or that he had offered a million dollars for it. Yet another rumor was that RKO were intending to reshoot some of the film's scenes in order to "tone it down." Welles, furious upon hearing this, said if it were true he would take action. . . .

... The Kane-Hearst-Welles-RKO battle was drawing to its close. The Hearst press made one final attack and lapsed into hurt silence. This latest attack was, perhaps, the most senseless yet perpetrated.

BOLSHEVIK BOGEY

In early 1941, a few American authors came together to form The Free Company whose object was, by means of the radio play, to remind the American people of their natural rights and of the value of those rights. It evolved that they would follow the method of the Bible parable or of the fables of Æsop and present a series of plays each of which would deal with one of the basic civil rights of the American citizen or with the general aspect of the whole subject of freedom. Each play was to be written by a leading writer, and stars of stage, screen, and radio were to be asked to appear in them. No one was to be paid, and the Company was, in its organizer's words, "a group of Americans, unsponsored and uncontrolled, expressing as a voluntary act of faith our belief in our fundamental institutions."

The CBS gave The Free Company air space and those who contributed plays included William Saroyan, Marc Connelly, Robert E. Sherwood, James Boyd, Stephen Vincent Benét, Paul Green, Archibald MacLeish, Maxwell Anderson, and the late Sherwood Anderson. A play, the sixth in the Company's series, called *His Honor, The Mayor* by Orson Welles, was broadcast on April 6, 1941.

From any point of view, *His Honor, The Mayor* was not an outstanding piece of radio-craft. It was in the usual Wellesian style by having the action progressed mainly by dialogue with a minimum of sound effects and music, the whole presided over by Welles as narrator and producer. Welles claimed in his introduction that he was offering no message or moral, was trying to be neither uplifting nor inspirational. The play told how the Mayor (played by Ray Collins) overcame the first expressions of fascism—a league called The White Crusaders —in a small town on the Mexican border by abusing at no point any of the rights of the citizen—such as the right to hold opinions or the right to congregate. The Mayor was of no particular political color, save an upholder of the Bill of Rights and Lincoln's famous precept. Ranged against him were the ignorance and prejudice of the masses and the stealthy subversiveness of fascism and anti-Semitism. At the end, he overcomes both.

The next day, however, with all banners flying, the Hearst press rushed into battle loudly proclaiming The Free Company "Communistic" and attackers of the "American way of life." It was realized by everyone that the attack was directed primarily against Welles under the guise of criticism of The Free Company. It is beyond comprehension how anything supposedly "Communistic" was honestly found in *His Honor, The Mayor*—in which the only Communist is a harmless old man of eighty-seven. It was, it is true, a Socialist play in that it was written by a Socialist, but Welles carefully pointed out he was offering no opinion. He hoped, he said in the play, that people would think about the Mayor's problem and how he tackled it. He would, indeed, be very pleased to hear of listeners' thoughts on the subject.

The fuss, of course, died down almost as quickly as it arose. Some found it amusing to observe that Mr. Hearst's left hand knew not what his right hand was doing. Several of Mr. Hearst's radio stations regularly carried the broadcasts of The Free Company.

On April 8, Orson Welles was smuggled out of town, accompanied by his special physician, on whose orders he was retiring to a "private sanitorium," suffering from excessive fatigue. He was to rest for at least three weeks. He turned up at Palm Springs.

Citizen Kane was shown to the press simultaneously in the middle of the day on April 9, at the Broadway Theatre in New York and the Ambassador in Los Angeles. In New York, from a highly professional audience that contained many publishers and newspapermen, the film received an ovation. It looked very much indeed as if Orson Welles had done it again.

CITIZEN KANE

Reaction to the film *Citizen Kane* is so much a personal affair that to be dogmatic about it is to be both foolish and tolerant. The author's opinion, for what it is worth, is that, excepting the films of Chaplin which are essentially of no country at all but of the world, with Griffith's *Birth of a Nation* and *Intolerance,* some of the work of von Stroheim and a few other isolated films, *Citizen Kane* is the best and most important motion picture ever to be made in the USA. The word "greatness" which is so often abused should not, perhaps, be applied since it might imply treatment of an epic theme. The Welles film is hardly that, yet it gave the most searching and complete analysis ever made on film of an individual, imaginary or real. It succeeded in recreating as no other film has ever done, seventy years of American life in the most realistic and vivid manner. Its script is one of the most amazing ever written and is astounding in its compactness, conciseness, completeness, and complexity. It contains some of the most interesting and exciting technical contributions ever seen in a film which were, if not new, rediscoveries for the time. It contains some of the best acting ever seen on a screen. It is, above all, the creation of one man—*and it has style.*

The Script

The third revised final script of *Kane* by Orson Welles and Herman J. Mankiewicz, dated July 16, 1940—the script from which the film was shot—is one hundred and fifty-six pages in length: it runs, as a film, with the various changes made during production, for one hundred and nineteen minutes and represents 10,750 feet of film. In that time and length of film, all the relevant, outstanding facts of the life of a man who lived to be seventy-six are discovered, aired, and commented upon. The main story, after the Prologue and news-short, is told in flashbacks representing the facts learned by the reporter in his interviews with the people who knew Kane: the comments of these people on Kane are recorded in the present-day scenes during which the narrator and Thompson are together. Every interview yields some new fact or opinion, or presents some new light on an incident that has gone before. It is doubtful if there has ever been written a screenplay so complexly constructed as that for *Kane*. Even that for David Wark Griffith's *Intolerance,* which, although it was never actually written on paper, developed four stories all set in widely separated periods of history, progressed these stories entirely in a forward manner. Time in *Kane* means nothing chronologically speaking, yet means everything from the drama's point of view. The camera runs forward, backward, and sometimes sidesteps to pick up an extra thread: one episode may deal with Kane from boyhood to almost the end of his life (as did that related by Thatcher's memoirs) to be followed by another which may do the same or concentrate upon one particular incident or incidents in the man's life. Yet every scene is an integral part of the whole and to cut even a foot would mean that something significant was lost. The general effect of the film is not so much a gathering together of many both tiny and large threads to wield them as one momentous cataract at the picture's end as, for instance, did *Intolerance,* but of working on a huge canvas and adding stitches or daubs gradually until the whole becomes clear at the end, then to be viewed in perspective. It is like the jigsaw puzzles that are referred to in it: the prologue is somewhat mystifying and confusing, followed by the burst of enlightenment of the news-digest and then, by a steady and logical process of filling in the remaining pieces until, in the very last few feet of the film, Rosebud, the piece that was thought to be lost, suddenly goes into place so easily that it is wondered why it was not seen before. The puzzle is complete and resolved, revealing a picture of which previously had only been seen parts.

Mr. Terry Ramsaye suggested the technique derived largely from Luce's *Time* magazine, which endeavors to be "curt, concise, complete" with words. It is true that the film was like that: the moment a point had been made or an action explained, the camera is whipped off to show some other aspect which, although perhaps seen before, is presently paraded with further significance. For instance, Susan Alexander is first seen singing *Thaïs* with the camera angling upstage—i.e., from the audience's point of view, for this is the sequence derived from Leland's remarks, and it is he who is seeing it. Some time later we see the same incident (although now the last act of the opera), this time with the camera shooting towards the audience, for it is now Susan's viewpoint that we are learning.

The continuity by means of which the action and interest is transported from one place or from one time to another is equally involved, clever, and amazingly unobtrusive. Perhaps the best example of this in the film begins when Kane, having just met Susan, learns of her ambitions to sing and asks her to demonstrate her voice. In the dingy parlor of the house in which Susan lodges, she and Kane sit—she at the piano, he in a chair. She begins to sing in her tiny voice: the picture dissolves, although her voice continues as before, and it is now revealed that the scene is a larger, more "classy" private room, with Susan, more elaborately gowned, sitting this time at a grand piano, and Kane stretched luxuriously in a basket chair, at ease with the world. The scene, without a word being spoken, immediately tells a lot of Susan's and Kane's mutual relationship. Susan finishes her song; Kane, a happy smile on his face, applauds. The picture commences to dissolve once more and the clapping becomes that of several people: the new picture discloses Jedediah Leland (it is the episode in which he figures) in a small car outside the old *Inquirer* building, addressing a small group of people. Posters, plastered over surrounding walls, tell at a glance that Kane is running for a governorship. When the people have ceased to applaud him in their desultory manner, Leland starts to speak to them. After a few remarks he is saying: "He entered on this campaign . . ." when there is a quick dissolve and immediately, without waiting for this to complete itself, Kane's voice takes up the sentence, reverberating as if in a huge hall, ". . . with one purpose only!" and we are indeed in Madison Square Garden with Kane addressing his final rally audience. It is a beautiful sequence and one that is, it is interesting to note, not in the shooting script.

Of Welles's dialogue, little adverse criticism is possible: by either intuition or his acute perceptive powers, every phrase in the script is beautifully turned and pointed, is remarkably in character, and, above all, is natural. The whole film depends mainly on its dialogue to further the action (or, better, the thought *behind* the action, since the film is a state of mind) rather than any essentially cinematic movement. However, since the film is a biography, this was the only justifiable course; in any man's life, conversation and speech play a far greater part than anything which may be called "cinematic action." *Kane* is, as well as being a narrative, a reporting of a man's life—a life spent mainly thinking and talking about himself—and an inherent psychological analysis of the man's character. Ramsaye described it very well as the "intensely graphic vivisection of an hypothesis." Thus the film is, most certainly, in that style called "theatrical," but it is also, probably, the best "talkie" yet realized. The sound, besides the dialogue, is beautifully designed and integrated with thought and action.

In general, it is selective and used only to underline a point, further the continuity and/or to give an impression of realism. There is that thrilling moment when Kane, refusing to leave Susan's apartment with his wife and Gettys, rushes on to the landing to scream after his rival: "I'm going to send you to Sing Sing, Gettys. Sing Sing! Sing ———" but by this time Gettys reaches and closes the front door and, instead of the last word of Kane's sentence, there is the tiny, mocking "peep" of a distant car. Again, there is the scene at the Everglades camp to which Kane has dragged his retinue for a "picnic." In their tent, Kane and Susan are fiercely quarrelling; he has just slapped her across the face. During the ensuing dialogue, a woman screams half-hysterically, half in a reckless amusement, off scene, the noise rising to its climax after Kane says, "I'm not sorry," just before the scene fades out.

More obvious, but equally startling, is the point at which Raymond picks up the threads. As his narrative begins, Susan, at the time she is leaving Kane, marches on to and across the terrace on her way to the car. Far below are the waters of the Gulf Coast. Almost before the scene has dissolved in and Susan has entered the frame on the right, a gorgeous tropical bird rises, startled, immediately in front of the camera and gives an ear-splitting screech.

Music is used in like interesting fashion—not as an added accompaniment or needless imitation of a natural sound, but deliberately to provoke mood and atmosphere. It begins in the very first few feet when it commentates upon the scenes as the camera draws nearer to the palace in the murky dawn. At the end of that journey, with the frame occupied by a close-up of the lighted window, the light within the room goes out. Immediately, not only does this stop the forward movement of the camera, but also cuts dead the music. It is almost as if one were tiptoeing in forbidden grounds (the notice on the fence had said: PRIVATE—NO TRESPASSING) when suddenly a sound, or an action (such as the light being extinguished) causes one to immobilize completely and hardly dare to breathe. In the perfect stillness, the frozen atmosphere is accentuated by the reflection in the window panes of the dreary estate and dawn sky. Then, when things are patently safe, the action starts up again and the camera finds itself within the room—Charles Foster Kane's bedroom. The diffused light of the just-rising sun breaks through the window and with it the music rises up again, almost as if with relief. There follows that incredible snow scene with the "big impossible flakes, the too picturesque farmhouse and snowman," and, in Welles's own words, "the jingling of sleigh bells in the musical score now makes an ironic reference to Indian Temple bells—the music freezes—" and Kane whispers, "Rosebud!"

Two good examples in which the music and sound are almost "stylized" are, firstly, that when the frantic rush of preparations for the opera is becoming too much for Susan: music, voices, sound all rise up to a tremendous peak and, as an electric light bulb flutters and fades, suddenly trail miserably away, whereupon the scene dissolves in on Susan's attempted suicide. Secondly, there is that scene in which Leland, immediately after Kane's terrible defeat at the polls, gets drunk and staggers towards the *Inquirer* building: a man is turning the handle of an hurdy-gurdy and on the sound track, barely audible, is the song that had been written for Kane many years before—"Oh, Mr. Kane!"—played slowly, mournfully, as a dirge. It is a wonderfully pathetic scene made doubly so by remembrance of the song's words, heard only before in such different, joyous circumstances. Slowly do they return themselves to the watcher's mind—"There is a man, a certain man, who for the poor, you may be sure, will do all he can. . . ."

Direction

Citizen Kane was, it must be remembered, the first motion picture with which Orson Welles had been in any way connected, save for the two abortive scripts which preceded it.[3] It revealed him to be one of the most skillful, brilliant, and perceptive directors in the world.

There is the hint of Welles's theatrical origins, as has been said, in certain aspects of the script; beyond that, he might have spent years evolving his art, as did many less important directors, in the oppressive atmosphere of Hollywood. One thing is important to recall: Welles had accomplished much on the radio. He had developed a personal technique that was to show more in *The Magnificent Ambersons* than it did in his first picture, yet the point is that acting and direction in the medium of radio call for a similar restraint as in cinema.

Welles had a wonderful unit, the chief member of which was undoubtedly his cameraman, Gregg Toland. With Toland, Welles spent

---

[3] [See the filmography in this volume, p. 169, for corrections resulting from recent scholarship.]

countless hours planning lighting, set-ups, and angles. Every shot in the film was most carefully built up and designed off the sound-stage, before it was taken. It is widely commented upon that *Citizen Kane* had a ceiling to practically every set. It is true that these ceilings gave added realism, intense mood, and some wonderful lighting effects, but they were not incorporated merely for their own sake. They were essential components of the method of photography that Toland developed under force of Welles's ideas and requirements. It arose from two main objections Welles had to conventional movie photography. The comparatively narrow angle of vision given by the camera lens usually in use compared not at all to the very wide angle given by the human eye: to relate that which is seen by the camera more closely to that seen by the eye is simply done by the use of a "wide-angle" lens. Secondly, Welles had no desire to use the conventional close-up. It was in his mind to tell more than one thing at a single camera set-up, so full of significant detail are his films.

The added field given by a wide-angle lens, however, would include the tops of the sets and the studio walls beyond, should the set wall be the usual nine-to-fifteen feet of the usual room. Therefore, it was essential the set should have a ceiling.

In a normal close-up, only the very close foreground is in focus— the rest is blurred and indistinct. If this further field is focussed, it results automatically that the foreground becomes out of focus, thus giving a very ugly picture in which much detail is lost. Toland, therefore, developed what he calls "pan focus" by which all three planes —fore-, mid- and background—are equally clear and discernible. The method again requires a wide-angle lens, a small aperture (on some of the scenes in *Kane* the aperture was stopped down to as much as $f11$) and one strong source of light.

There are many examples of the method in the film. When Susan attempts to commit suicide, the scene dissolves in on a bottle, spoon, and glass on a bedside table in the very near foreground, thus telling the complete story immediately. The center field, in which Susan actually lies in bed, is dark and not visible until the blinds are let up. The background is of the door, through which Kane bursts in, immediately taking in the situation. Thus, everything is told and observed with one set-up, obviating the need for desperate cutting, tracking, and close-ups by the camera. This scene is, as a matter of fact, one of Toland's favorites. A further example which contains some of the finest lighting in the film is that in which Kane is finishing the bad notice started by Leland. Kane is seated at a desk, typing, in the immediate left foreground, while behind him the camera takes in the whole length of the City Room. Through the door at the back of the room, Leland comes unsteadily forward, down the whole length of the long room to where Kane is working. It is a scene brilliant in its tenseness, compactness, and tautness.

One final example from the many the picture offers is that in which Signor Matisti, Susan's voice trainer, is giving her a lesson in Kane's New York house. In the right foreground, Susan stands holding a sheet of music; at the left is the piano player; while Matisti, in his shirtsleeves, stands at his side further from the camera. In the middle of the action, through the open door at the back, Kane enters and stands watching. There is thus a semicircle of figures, ranging in distance from immediately in front of the camera on the two sides to the very rear of the set in the middle, and all are in focus. The whole scene, about 200 feet in length, is played on this one set-up.

A further speciality in the camera work on the film was the choice, composition, and lighting of the angles. Generally, the camera was below eye level, shooting up. There is both a psychological and an artistically practical reason for this. To photograph a person or object from below inevitably distorts, be it ever so slightly, that object. It appears to elongate a person, making him, therefore, seem more important. Conversely, it in a sense intimidates the audience, since it is in the inferior position of looking up. The scene thus gives an added power to the person on the screen and exercises a minor hypnotic influence upon the audience. Another very good reason is that, with this particular angle, some remarkably fine photographic effects can be obtained, and were realised to the full in *Kane*. There is the scene in Kane's office when Leland comes to reprove him after the scandal. The two men, arguing, close together, are photographed from at their feet; the camera is at an approximate angle of thirty-five degrees to the vertical. It is a beautiful shot, with the camera swinging round almost as if on a pivot as it follows the men's actions. The set was, actually, built up off the floor of the stage, with Toland photographing it through a hole in the set floor. In order to record the sequence, the microphone and its boom were above the ceiling which, in the field of vision, was made of muslin. A perfect camera-angle is the set-up in the hall of Susan Alexander's apartment at the time of the election. The camera shoots steeply upwards from a point very close to the foot of the stairs towards the place where the stair rail meets that of the landing. The scene is beautifully lit. Gettys, a cynical smile on his face, comes deliberately and quietly down the stairs, pausing imperceptibly when he is nearest the camera, while, above him, leaning over the landing rail, Kane screams his abuse.

In a film in which every set-up has at least one point of interest, it is invidious and impossible to select many for examination. One, however, of very great interest, is that in the projection room, immediately after the *News on the March* has been run: the only light is that streaming through the projection ports, and that of a tiny desk lamp. In a scene in which only the dialogue matters, the attention is not distracted by facial expressions since none of the faces are illuminated by the available light. A sweep of an arm, a nod of the head, cutting a great, solid chunk of shadow, doubly emphasises a point. Toland actually shot this in one of the RKO Studio projection rooms: because his camera, for the most part, was shooting into blazing arcs, he used a special lens coating to cut "flare." Like Welles, he is mainly interested in creating realism and, wherever possible, he uses natural sources of light for illumination. The very great care taken in relating one frame-composition to its successor is also very noticeable. Even when a dissolve is in operation, a definite screen pattern is maintained, sometimes with remarkable results.

Welles has amazing power over his players, drawing from them performances they never give under another director. He is, to them, a mixture of tyrant, friend, and boy scout leader. They both love and fear him. Probably much of his great success with them comes from the fact that he has conceived the characters they are playing and, consequently, is intimately and entirely aware of their every action, thought, and glance. Being a brilliant actor himself he is able to demonstrate what he wants done: when his players are as capable as, say, Agnes Moorehead (who Welles says is "one of the greatest actresses in the world") or Ray Collins, no subtle nuance of direction is lost for the observant watcher. Nothing short of miraculous must be Welles's sense of timing, as so vividly demonstrated by the two films he has directed. This, coupled with his lifelike dialogue, gives a most amazing impression of reality. A good example is in the projection room sequence. The reel has been cut off and the music trails grotesquely away. An imperceptible pause and Thompson says, "That's it." He gets up and lights a cigarette, seating himself on the corner of the table: Rawlston and the Yes-man shift in their seats and light cigarettes. Then a man says into the phone, "Stand by. I'll tell you if we want to run it again." There is another slight pause until Thompson says, "Well?—How about it, Mr. Rawlston?" Rawlston rises and asks: "How do you like it, boys?"

A short silence is followed by three of the Yes-men starting to talk simultaneously. "Well—er—" says the first. "Seventy years of a man's life—" noncommits another. "That's a lot to try to get into a newsreel—" concludes the third. It is doubtful if there is another director in Hollywood who could write that sequence or, if written, could play it properly. But Welles captures the whole atmosphere and gives away the characters of Rawlston and the Yes-men, with a bit of Thompson's, all in a few feet of film. That is both economy and art.

More impressive, exciting, important, and amazing than any other sequence in the picture is that of the film within the film—the news digest short, *News on the March*. It is, undoubtedly, one of the most exciting single sequences ever filmed. Originally, in the script, it was intended to prepare one for the ensuing conventional unconventionality (for it is immediately preceded by Kane's death) by fading in on a projection room with the camera moving towards the screen, framing it completely as the titles appear. These were to be simply, "MAIN TITLE" and "CREDITS." However, it will be remembered that in the film, with no preliminaries, the short's frame is identical with that of the main film and, with brassy music playing, there appears the title, "News on the March" followed by "Obituary: Xanadu's Landlord." The sequence is difficult to comment upon since its practically sole attribute is the amazing manner in which reality has been created—not recreated as has only been done before. To this must be added the manner in which a seemingly authentic digest, in the style of, say, *The March of Time*, was made. There is no shot in it that might not have been taken, with a period camera and processed by period printers, at the time the event was supposed to happen, filed in a library and cut into a reel prepared after the man's death.

When Kane is speaking in 1916 on a platform outside the *Inquirer* building, the light flickers, the film jumps, and the "rain" pelts down. The shot is silent (but is run at sound speed) and is therefore followed by a title—the so familiar type of title of white lettering on black background. When Thatcher is appearing before a Congressional Investigation Committee in a newsreel shot, there is the bad lighting, the natural and disorderly grouping of people, and the hum on the sound track, all so patently authentic. This was, actually, a reproduction of the existing newsreel on J. P. Morgan.

Some of the reconstructed newsreel shots are later seen in the body of the picture as the "real thing." For instance, the shot of Susan and Kane leaving the City Hall after their marriage is seen both in the shot and in the sequence narrated by Leland.

There are many other bits in the digest that are astounding in their "rightness"—the shots of Xanadu building in the twenties; Kane being burned in effigy by a night crowd; the Clipper interview with Kane; the "bootlegged" shots of the old man at Xanadu in the thirties; the titles—as for instance:

> To forty-four million U.S. news buyers, more newsworthy than the names in his own headlines, was Kane himself, greatest newspaper tycoon of this or any other generation;

the funeral at Xanadu and, at the very end of the sequence, the moving sign on the *Inquirer* building in New York: "CHARLES FOSTER KANE—DEAD."

The sequence can only be called, as are some pieces of music, "an exercise in the style of . . ." and it is an exercise that is wholly successful. Everything—scripting, commentary and its delivery, photography, lighting, and acting—is correct. Only an Orson Welles could have done it. Not even Louis de Rochemont, the originator and developer of the *March of Time,* was as wholly successful in combining reality and fiction in his own *The House on 92nd Street.*

Acting and General Production

Citizen Kane brought to the screen a whole new school of film acting. A few films before it had begun to explore the path but *Kane* brought the style to perfection. Without doubt, Welles gave one of the greatest performances ever registered on film. He is, in any case, a very accomplished actor, but it is important to remember that he conceived, developed, and lived with Charles Foster Kane for many months. He knew his every thought, action, and desire so that it was inevitable he should become identified completely with him. It is hardly likely that the film is at all autobiographical except, perhaps, in one respect. The revelation of Rosebud shows Kane died thinking of his childhood. Although the reporter has proved that neither one word nor one incident can explain a man's life, it means Kane's childhood, or rather, his memory of it, had played a large subconscious part in making him that which he was. Kane had little family life, but just enough to cause him to have, in his maturity, sweet memories of it and a regret he had no more. When he meets Susan—"a cross-section of the American public"—that night in 1915, he tells her, "I was on my way—in search of my youth." His dead mother's things had been stored in a warehouse that he was now visiting for the first time on "a sort of sentimental journey." Taken from his parents, whom he both loved, at the age of five, he grew up in the care of a bank. This undoubtedly had a great influence on his life, yet could hardly have produced his fundamental trait of, as Leland tells him, "not caring about anything except you. You just want to convince people that you love them so much that they should love you back. Only you want love on your own terms." And Kane later replies, "A toast, Jedediah —to love on *my* terms. Those are the only terms anybody knows—his own." On the other hand, so sexless and warmthless a childhood would most certainly have intensified, and perhaps brought out, a possibly latent egocentricity. Welles himself had no orthodox childhood. Deprived of a mother from an early age, he travelled widely and was treated as an adult. There may have been moments in *Citizen Kane* that were Welles yearning for a more normal childhood.

Physically, there is no doubt that Charles Foster Kane lives and ages before the audience's eyes. The makeup was by Maurice Seiderman, whom Welles styles "the greatest makeup man in the world," and is miraculously achieved and successful. Sixteen each of different chins, jowls, ears, hairlines, necks, lips, cheeks, noses, and eyesacs were designed in keeping with Kane's age. His eyes change with the years, becoming pale and veined: the effect was brought about by the use of contact lens. The flabbiness that the middle- and old-aged man assumes is a simulation of actual flesh, built up by means of a synthetic rubber prepared by Seiderman himself.

In a cast of brilliant players, all of whom gave their best, it is invidious to select any for especial mention. Ray Collins, as Gettys, deserves it, for his was a beautiful performance. The incomparable Agnes Moorehead as the mother, Mrs. Kane, was also outstanding. The difficult part of Susan was played by Dorothy Comingore—a discovery of Chaplin's—with great distinction and ability. On the same high level were Joseph Cotten as Leland, Everett Sloane as Bernstein, and George Coulouris as Thatcher. Just how much their performances were due to Welles is suggested by comparison with later ones under different directors. Agnes Moorehead has never surpassed her performance in *Kane* and that to follow in *The Magnificent Ambersons* by anything she has done as an MGM contract player. The same may be said of the others. Welles must get these performances from his cast by endless, patient rehearsal, his impressive, dominating personality, and his natural gift of split-second timing. As a great actor, he knows how a state of mind may be expressed by physical actions.

It has been remarked that *Citizen Kane* cost only $746,000, including cast salaries but excluding any payment to Welles. For such an ambitious production, the figure is amazingly small: there are many sets, some of which are quite sizeable; there are many trick and model shots; there is a large cast and expensive unit. Throughout the preparations and production, however, Welles and his associates strove for economy in all things provided it was not at the picture's expense. The classic example of an economy shot which obviated a very conventional scene is that supposedly in the Chicago Opera House when, the scene taken from Susan's angle, the camera shoots past her into what is a crowded auditorium. As it would be in reality, the auditorium is a black, unfathomable void from which shines a multitude of front-of-house spots. The scene was shot by building up a stage and proscenium at one end of a sound-stage and arranging 160 baby-spots before it as the f.o.h. lights. With the camera angling directly into this empty stage and applause dubbed in on the sound track, a perfect illusion of reality is obtained at comparatively negligible expense.

Kane was so wholly personal a creation as to restrict its immediate effect upon other films to insignificant details. For other writers or directors to acknowledge too closely its effect upon them might have produced whispered charges of plagiarism. However, there is little doubt but that it exerted a wide influence over the movie colony. When playing in Hollywood, where it stayed for many weeks, it was no unusual thing for professionals to outnumber nonprofessionals in the audience. Various effects deriving from the films, which were profuse after its release, were, for instance, the use of wide-angle lens and consequently ceilings, new methods of continuity, a more fluid camera, "arty" lighting, queer angles, murky photography, more natural acting and dialogue. The complex script, which itself had its origins in the "narratage" of Preston Sturges' *The Power and the Glory* (Fox-Lasky, 1933), was not imitated at all. *Kane* was unusual in that it was sufficient unto itself. Its effect was not so much in the nature of a technical stimulus, but a mental one. Like *Das Cabinet des Dr. Caligari* (1919), its main effect was to reinforce a conviction in the wonderful untapped resources of the film medium, without starting a whole new school of cinematography. The most admirable thing in it—its superb, uncompromising realism—is too dangerous a thing for Hollywood to wish to imitate widely.

Citizen Kane remains, today, Welles's greatest accomplishment in any medium. Mature, real, brilliant—an artistic entity. It is doubtful if, although yet so young, he will ever be in a position to surpass it, for it was made without any supervision or interference by the studio. Insistent to be granted full and complete freedom in his contract, he demanded it when his film was on the floor. The story is told of how, one day, two top RKO executives visited his set unannounced and without prior arrangements. Welles, furious, told his cast and unit to start a baseball game, left the stage and refused to come back until the visitors had departed, baffled and raging. The incident could hardly have improved his relations with the "front office," most of the members of which, throughout his stay on the lot, insisted he was a madman, driving the company to ruin.

He knows how much ground he has lost: "I came to Hollywood saying, 'If they let me do a second picture, I'm lucky.' They didn't, and since that time I've been trying to get back to the position I was in when I first arrived with a contract to make the picture in my own way without interference."

"It's Terrific!"

Citizen Kane had its world première at the New York Palace—onetime home of top-name vaudeville—on the evening of Thursday, May

1, 1941. Welles, back from Palm Springs, attended with Dolores del Rio. RKO had wanted to open the film at two New York theatres—at the Palace on a two-shows-a-day, advanced-admissions policy and at another hall with continuous performances. The second cinema being unobtainable, only the Palace played it on its arranged system. The façade of the theatre, the decoration of which cost $26,000, consisted of a series of neon signs of Welles gradually mounting in size, which, illuminated separately and in rapid succession, gave the impression of a growing figure. Above this, another huge sign proclaimed, "IT'S TERRIFIC!" and the whole was wreathed in steam from two jets in the theatre's canopy. Practically all the New York, with some Hollywood executives of the major companies and the more famous members of New York's café society, attended the opening.

The lay press of New York was generally impressed, but also puzzled. Bosley Crowther in the *New York Times* suggested Welles had created a titanic character which did everything but explain itself. Eileen Creelman in the *Sun* decided the film was "an interesting one, with a decided personality all its own. . . . But . . . it is a cold picture, a puzzle rather than a drama. . . . The interest is only intellectual, not dramatic."

The first week, it played to capacity business, grossing $30,000 with $10,000 in advance from booked seats. Business dropped off sharply subsequently and the film finished, after nine weeks at the theatre, with a generally disappointing gross.

Other towns had test showings: Chicago at the Woods and Palace; Washington at Keith's; Los Angeles at the Hillstreet and El Capitan; San Francisco at the Golden Gate. The Hollywood première was on May 8 at the El Capitan; business was stimulating in these situations: in practically all the large towns it played, the film was well received.

RKO had spent some $53,000 on advertising before the première in New York alone. All the papers carried reviews and advertisements with the exception of the Hearst papers, which ignored the film entirely. Welles told his friends that both in Palm Springs and Hollywood, he was being subjected to "mysterious efforts to invade his privacy." His draft board was solicited by male and female journalists who wished to learn his telephone number, details of his private life and why he had not been called up. He had, incidentally, been rejected by the U.S. Army as suffering from asthma, sinus trouble, a variety of allergies, and "inverted" flat feet.

On the coast, at this time, an "alien radical," Harry Bridges, was being tried with a view to his deportation. Welles, as a defender of freedom, formed a "Citizen's Committee for Harry Bridges" to support him. Involved with him were many notable intellectuals and thinkers, including university professors. With one bound, the Hearst press took up the ancient scent, revelling in this new indication of Welles's "communistic" beliefs. Beyond a joke and beyond contempt, the ridiculous campaign was ignored by those against whom it was directed.

Citizen Kane was roadshown throughout America in the summer of 1941, and made available for general release in RKO's Block 5 of that year: the release date was September 5. On its trip to the rural areas and small towns of America, the film suffered badly. For several months, the "What the Picture Did For Me" department of the *Motion Picture Herald* contain plaintive cries from isolated exhibitors about what the picture did for them. The fault was not entirely that of the film. Many exhibitors and circuits preferred to pay for the film, which they acquired in an RKO block, but not to show it—writing off the rental as a dead loss. For instance, the Fox West Coast Theatres bought it but would not show it. RKO, let it be recorded, undertook to play the film in each locality where the circuit refused to. For some of those who did show it, however, the name of Orson Welles occurred frequently in their subsequent nightmares. As C. A. Lejeune remarked, some time afterwards, "Exhibitors still gather round the fire on winter evenings, and tell their children grim, ghastly tales of their experiences with *Citizen Kane*."

When the film came to London in October 1941, the reception was almost identical to that it had experienced in America. Critical acclaim —relative financial failure. The fate of many an outstanding film in the past fifty years.

It was selected as the best picture of 1941 by both the National Board of Review and the New York Critics' Circle, and was expected to figure prominently among the winners of the Academy of Motion Picture Arts and Sciences' "Oscars." It received only an award for the year's best Original Screenplay: Welles looks back on the incident rather ruefully. "I was nominated for just about everything the Academy had to offer. I was in Rio at the time and the press interviewed me and made much of the occasion and asked for statements on how I felt winning so many awards. I just barely made it as a writer when the announcements were made."

CITIZEN KANE:
The American Baroque
by ANDREW SARRIS

The recent revival of *Citizen Kane* has not elicited the kind of reappraisal the occasion demands. It is too easy to dismiss *Kane* as a great film with the smug confidence that everything that is to be said about it has already been said. If nothing else, the fifteen years that have elapsed since its initial release should provide a new perspective. The fact that *Citizen Kane* still seems to be ahead of its time is as much an indictment of contemporary filmmaking as it is a vindication of the classical quality of its art. Stripped of its personal and topical sensationalism, the film has risen above the capricious attacks leveled against it fifteen years ago.

A great deal of the hostility aroused by *Kane* back in 1941 was directed at its youthful creator, Orson Welles. Many of his enemies have since been appeased by the simple fact that Welles has joined the mortal herd by getting fifteen years older. Others have come to admire his dogged professionalism in the face of disastrously inadequate financing and even personal injury as demonstrated by his recent performance of *Lear* from a wheelchair. Yet, though tempered by adversity and voluntary exile, the spectacular Welles personality still obscures the more substantial aspects of his genius.

On a less personal level, *Citizen Kane* disappointed many who were caught up in the portentous political atmosphere of 1941. Advance publicity had prepared many liberals for a savage political attack on William Randolph Hearst, one of the most prominent enemies of the New Deal. *The Grapes of Wrath* and *The Great Dictator*, both released in 1940, had made their stands at the barricades. Welles himself

"*Citizen Kane: The American Baroque*" by Andrew Sarris. From Film Culture 2 (1956): 14–16. Reprinted by permission of Film Culture and the author.

had recently mounted an antifascist interpretation of *Julius Caesar* on the New York stage. The boycott of Welles and *Citizen Kane* by all Hearst publications further heightened the suspense that there would be a collision between the *enfant terrible* of the left and grand old man of the right.

When *Kane* finally appeared, it failed to justify all the ideological anticipation. Charles Foster Kane was not William Randolph Hearst in any "significant" sense. Welles and Herman J. Mankiewicz had merely borrowed biographical details, some virtually libelous, to fashion an intricate screenplay that posed a psychological mystery without advancing any cause.

After subtracting the criticism of the Welles personality and the criticism of the lack of ideology, all that is left and all that is relevant is the criticism of *Citizen Kane* as a work of art. To believe, as some do, that *Citizen Kane* is the great American film, it is necessary to produce an interpretation that answers some of the more serious objections to this film.

Citizen Kane has peculiar claims to greatness in that its distinctive merits are related to its alleged flaws. Adverse criticism of *Kane* is based mainly on three propositions: (1) its narrative structure is unduly complicated; (2) its technique calls attention to itself; (3) its intellectual content is superficial.

If any one of these propositions is fully accepted, *Kane* falls far short of greatness. At first glance, all three points have some validity. The narrative zigzags and backtracks to its conclusion. The technique dazzles the eye and ear. No profound ideas are explicitly developed. A closer examination of the film, however, reveals an inner consistency of theme, structure, and technique. The implications of this consistency are crucial to any effective analysis of what *Citizen Kane* is really about.

Within the maze of its own aesthetic, *Kane* develops two interesting themes: the debasement of the private personality of the public figure, and the crushing weight of materialism. Taken together, these two themes comprise the bitter irony of an American success story that ends in futile nostalgia, loneliness, and death. The fact that the personal theme is developed verbally while the materialistic theme is developed visually creates a distinctive stylistic counterpoint. Against this counterpoint, the themes unfold within the structure of a mystery story.

Charles Foster Kane dies in a lonely castle. His last word is *"Rosebud."* Who or what is *Rosebud?* This is the mystery of *Citizen Kane.* The detective is a reporter for a news service which produces *March of Time*-like newsreels. The suspects are all the persons and objects Kane encountered in his cluttered life. The clues are planted in the film on three occasions, but, unlike the conventional mystery key, *Rosebud* is the answer to a man's life rather than his death. And since the intangible meanings of life end in the mystery of death, *Rosebud* is not the final solution but only the symbolic summation.

Rosebud is the means through which the past history of Charles Foster Kane is penetrated by the reporter-detective and the omniscient camera. Time is thrown back and brought forward in the four major movements of the film, the flashback-recollections respectively of Kane's banker-guardian, his business manager, his best friend, and his second wife. Each major flashback begins at a later point in time than its predecessor, but each flashback overlaps with at least one of the others so that the same event or period is seen from two or three points of view.

There is a fifth flashback—a newsreel of Kane's public career— which establishes the identity of Charles Foster Kane for the first time in the film. There is no transition between the opening scene of a man dying in a lonely castle with *Rosebud* on his lips and the startling appearance of the unframed newsreel. This is the first shock effect in *Citizen Kane,* and it has received undeserved abuse as a spectacularly devious method of narration. What has been generally overlooked is the great economy of this device in establishing the biographical premises of the film without resorting to traditional montages of public reactions and telescoped historical events in the major movements of the story.

By isolating the newsreel from the main body of his film, Welles frees his flashbacks from the constricting demands of exposition, enabling his main characters to provide insights on the external outlines of the Kane biography. After the newsreel, the transitions are worked out very carefully through the logical movements of the reporter-detective. This shadowy, though thoroughly professional, character links the present to the past in an interlocking jigsaw puzzle with one elusive piece—*Rosebud*—appearing only at the very end in the reporter's absence since his services are no longer needed.

The newsreel accomplishes more than a skeletal public biography of Charles Foster Kane. On a narrative level, it introduces Mr. Thatcher, Kane's banker-guardian, whose memoirs will provide the first personal flashback of Kane's life and the first significant clue to *Rosebud.* The newsreel also produces a paradox that previsions the nonpolitical quality of the film. While Thatcher is telling a Committee that Kane is a Communist, a speaker in Union Square attacks Kane as a Fascist. The elderly Kane tells newsreel audiences that he is and always has been an American. This is the first indication that Kane is not really committed to any cause but Kane.

The newsreel fades out; a sudden establishing shot picks up a darkened projection room. The first of the many disembodied voices in the film calls out from the darkness, and the shadow plot of *Citizen Kane* begins. A group of cynical newsmen discuss ways of pepping up the newsreel. The reporter is sent out to find the secret of *Rosebud*. The semicolloquial dialogue is driven forth with relentless persistence from every direction. There is nothing profound or witty about any of it but it moves quickly and economically.

The reporter begins his search and the major movements of *Citizen Kane* begin. Through a hard, wide-angle lens, the reporter enters a cavernous museum, a dingy nightclub, a solidly upholstered office, a drab hospital ward, the gloomy mansion of Charles Foster Kane. The reporter's world is functional, institutional; an aging, weathered gateway to the life and time of Charles Foster Kane.

The sixth and last flashback of *Citizen Kane* offers the final clue to *Rosebud* and brings the reporter's quest to its unsuccessful conclusion. Interestingly enough, the three clues to *Rosebud* appear at times when Kane is being treated most remotely—in the cryptic death scene in the beginning, in the unfriendly memoirs of his banker-guardian, and in the final flashback narration of a cynical butler. The narrations of his closest acquaintances yield no clues to the symbolic truth of his life. This is the ultimate confirmation of Kane's spiritual loneliness, and it is upon this loneliness that the mystery structure of the film is based.

The mystery of *Rosebud* is solved in a memorable manner. The reporter and his entourage have departed from the Kane castle. As the cynical butler is directing the disposal of Kane's "junk" into the furnace, a workman picks up a sled in routine haste and dumps it into the flames. The camera closes in on the surface of the sled and the name *Rosebud* as the letters are dissolving in liquid fire. The audience is given the solution with the added knowledge that no one living on the screen will ever know the secret of *Rosebud*.

This solution has been attacked as a trick ending unworthy of its theme. Yet without this particular resolution, the film would remain a jumbled jigsaw puzzle. The burning sled is apt not only as a symbolic summation but as a symbolic revelation. The reporter, the butler, the workman, the friends, the enemies, the acquaintances of Kane never discover *Rosebud* because it is lost amid the "junk" of Kane's materialistic existence.

Kane's tragedy lies in the inability of the props of experience to compensate for the bare emotional stage of his human relationships. Charles Foster collected valuable treasures from all over the world, but his last thoughts were of a sled he used as a boy before great wealth came into his life. At one point in the film, he tells his banker-guardian that he might have been a great man if he had not been so wealthy. *Rosebud* became the focal point of his nostalgia for a different turning point in his life. Kane's view of his own life is deterministic, and Kane's image throughout the film is remarkably consistent with this sense of determinism.

The apparent intellectual superficiality of *Citizen Kane* can be traced to the shallow quality of Kane himself. Even when Kane is seen as a crusading journalist battling for the lower classes, overtones of stiff self-idolatry mar his actions. His clever ironies are more those of the exhibitionist than the crusader. His best friend—a detached observer functioning as a sublimated conscience—remarks to the reporter that Kane never gave anything away: "he left you a tip." His second wife complained that Kane never gave her anything that was part of him, only material possessions that he might give a dog. His business adviser and lifelong admirer expressed the other side of Kane's personality when he observed that Kane wanted something more than money.

In each case, Kane's character is described in materialistic terms. What Kane wanted—love, emotional loyalty, the unspoiled world of his boyhood symbolized by *Rosebud*—he was unable to provide to those about him, or buy for himself. It is therefore fitting that the story of Kane should begin with his lonely death and conclude with the immolation of his life symbol.

The technique of Welles and his photographer, Gregg Toland, justifies the narrative structure. Apparently outrageous effects fall into place once the pattern of the film is discernible. *Kane* opens on a solid wire fence with a sign reading "No Trespassing." The camera moves up on a painted castle against a background of dark, brooding clouds. The same shots are repeated in reverse at the very end of the film. This initial and concluding clash of realism and expressionism flanks one of the most stylistically varied of all films.

The opening shots have been attacked as pretentious and the closing shots as anticlimactic. Yet, in a subtle way, the beginning and end of *Citizen Kane* suggest its theme. The intense material reality of the fence dissolves into the fantastic unreality of the castle and, in the end, the mystic pretension of the castle dissolves into the mundane substance of the fence. Matter has come full circle from its original quality to the grotesque baroque of its excess.

As each flashback unfolds, the visual scenario of *Citizen Kane* orchestrates the dialogue. A universe of ceilings dwarfs Kane's personal stature. He becomes the prisoner of his possessions, the ornament of his furnishings, the fiscal instrument of his collections. His booming voice is muffled by walls, carpets, furniture, hallways, stairs, and vast recesses of useless space.

Toland's camera set-ups are designed to frame characters in the oblique angles of light and shadow created by their artificial environment. There are no luminous close-ups in which faces are detached from their backgrounds. When characters move across rooms, the floors and ceilings move with them, altering the points of reference but never transcending them. This technique draws attention to itself both because it is so unusual and because it tends to dehumanize characters by reducing them to fixed ornaments in a shifting architecture.

Sound montage is used intensively within the flashbacks to denote the interval of time within two related scenes. A character will begin a sentence and complete it weeks, months, or years later in a different location. On occasion, one character will begin the sentence and another will complete it in the same manner. This device results in a constriction of time and an elimination of transitional periods of rest and calm. Aside from the aesthetic dividends of pacing and highlighting, *Kane*'s sound montage reinforces the unnatural tension of the central character's driving, joyless ambition. In all respects, *Kane*'s technique is a reflection and projection of the inhuman quality of its protagonist.

One brilliant use of sound montage that has generally been ignored as a piece of aural gargoyle is the piercing scream of a parakeet that precedes the last appearance of Kane in the film. One flashback and several scenes previously, Kane and his second wife are arguing in a tent surrounded by hundreds of Kane's picnic guests. A shrill scream punctuates the argument with a persistent, sensual rhythm. It is clear that some sexual outrage is being committed. When the parakeet screams at the appearance of Kane, the sound linkage in tone but not in time further dehumanizes Kane's environment. In the baroque world that he has created, Kane is isolated from even the most dubious form of humanity.

Kane's lack of humanity is consistently represented in the performance of Orson Welles, who alters the contours of Kane's rigidity from youth to old age. As a young man, Kane is peculiarly joyless. A gala occasion is recalled in which Kane threw a party for his new writers hired away from a competing newspaper. A group of chorus girls come on the scene. Kane is thrown in their midst and begins cutting up. The scene is heavy with Kane's studied posturing as the life of the party.

The acting in *Kane* emerges as an elaborate arabesque of interrupted conversations, harsh dissonances, and awkward physical confrontations. Kane's world, peopled by Mercury Players, is tuned to the egocentric performance of Welles. Joseph Cotten, Everett Sloane, and Dorothy Comingore, as Kane's best friend, business adviser, and second wife, respectively, and the main narrators of the film, achieve a strident rapport with the demanding presence of Welles. The intense pitch of the acting charges each line of dialogue with unexpected meanings. The manner of expression often alters the verbal content toward a new level of self-conscious cynicism. In this, the acting evokes the intentional hypocrisy of the few protestations of principle that appear in the script.

Towards the end of his life, Kane reacts to the desertion of his second wife by wrecking the furniture in her room. Again, his violent actions are rigidly controlled by a chilling self-awareness. As he is completing his unduly methodical havoc, he comes upon a crystal paperweight in which a minute snowstorm beats down on a miniature cottage. He speaks the name of *Rosebud* and walks past an array of guests across the path of endless mirrors and endless reflections of his image—mere repetitions of his ego without magnification. This is the final arithmetic of Kane's life, the last material accounting of his greatness.

Citizen Kane presents an intense vision of American life, distorting and amplifying its materialistic elements at the expense of human potentialities. The implied absence of free will in the development of Kane's character is thematically consistent with the moral climate of his environment. Kane's magnitude, unchecked by limiting principles or rooted traditions, becomes the cause of his spiritual ruin. Kane emerges as an extension of the nouveau-riche American seeking a living culture in the dead relics of the past. Striving desperately to transcend his material worth, Kane is victimized by the power his wealth possesses to alter the moral quality of his actions. In the end, everything has been bought and paid for, but nothing has been felt.

The Study of a Colossus
by PETER COWIE

> "We can get Kane out of our minds, but not Kane's dream."
> —WILLIAM WHITEBAIT

Citizen Kane is above all the study of a personality. It is not, as critics have often been led to assert, a frontal attack on the monopolies of American big business and politics (as is, say, Robert Rossen's *All the King's Men* or Elia Kazan's *A Face in the Crowd*); nor is it the study of a man's mind and private preoccupations (as is, say, Ingmar Bergman's *Wild Strawberries*). Kane remains a personality whose eminence and publicity depend solely on his ability to project his own magniloquent image; he becomes a symbol ("Few private lives were more public," booms the newsreel). The fact that he is a press magnate helps to counterpoint the excessive publicity he achieves, but is no more vital to the theme than "Rosebud" itself. His life and influence are seen not through his own eyes, but through those of other people. The entire film is a major reportage (without using the term in its pejorative sense), an enlargement and extension of the newsreel at the beginning. Thus the flashback method employed by Welles and Mankiewicz is vital to the success of the film. Mankiewicz's previous work had demonstrated his interest in biography, and in a narrative style that aimed at objectivity by accounting for several, often quite disparate viewpoints.

Kane is all things to all men. To Welles himself, "Kane is a man who abuses the power of the popular press and also sets himself up against the law, against the entire tradition of liberal civilization" [1]

"*The Study of a Colossus.*" From The Cinema of Orson Welles *by Peter Cowie (London and New York: Zwemmer and A. S. Barnes, 1965), pp. 21–37. Copyright © by Beaux Livres, S. A. Reprinted by permission of the author and the Successors of Beaux Livres, S. A.*

[1] André Bazin, Charles Bitsch, and Jean Domarchi, "Nouvel entretien avec Orson Welles," *Cahiers du Cinema*, no. 87 (September 1958).

and "at once egotistical and disinterested . . . at once an idealist and a swindler, a very great man and a mediocre individual."[2] To Thatcher, his erstwhile guardian, in his statement to the press, he is "nothing more or less—a communist" and a ruthless egotist who does not know how to handle money; rather more than a spoilt child. To the newsreel compilers and to "forty-four million news readers," he is a colossal, larger-than-life tycoon who dominated four decades of American life. To Susan, his mistress and subsequent wife, he appears as an awesome monster who launched her on her disastrous career as a singer without even asking her permission; mean, materialistic, and incapable of loving anyone. To Leland, his college friend, he is cynical and faintly malevolent ("he never gave you anything, he just left you a tip") and "always trying to prove something." To Bernstein, his General Manager, he was perhaps most congenial, "a man who lost nearly everything he had," a man to be pitied and revered.

(It is interesting to note by the way that Welles's own mentor in youth was a certain Doctor Bernstein who presented him, among other things, with a puppet theatre when he was in his infancy.)

To Raymond, his calculating *major domo* at Xanadu, Kane is a pathetic old fool. To himself, Kane is quite simply a wholly *autonomous* man. "There's only one person in this world who decides what I'm going to do, and that's me" he tells Emily in the scene with Gettys in Susan's rooms. When his newspapers are hit by the 1929 depression he says to Thatcher and Bernstein, "If I hadn't been very rich, I might have been a great man." Yet with the years this honesty of appraisal gradually vanishes. Kane weaves about himself a myth that ultimately even he acknowledges to be the truth; his fleeting references to "Rosebud" always emanate from his subconscious and so he can never quite grasp the exact nature of the lacuna that has prevented him from plotting an entirely satisfactory life. As André Bazin observed in this context, it is worth nothing to conquer the world if one has lost one's childhood.[3]

As if to make up for the loss of his beloved sledge, Kane devotes a major part of his life to the collection of material objects. He garners them omnivorously, from the world's biggest diamond ("I didn't know he was collecting diamonds," says Leland; "He's collecting someone who collects diamonds," replies Bernstein) to "the biggest private zoo since Noah." And all that he achieves through these acquisitions are manifold reflections of his own ego, symbolized in the mirror Kane limps past at Xanadu near the end. The statues and other artistic bric-à-brac of Xanadu suggest Kane's futile inability to *create*. Nothing

---

[2] Maurice Bessy, *Orson Welles, Cinema d'Aujourd'hui* Series no. 6 (Paris, 1963).
[3] André Bazin, *Orson Welles* (Paris, 1950).

remains after his death, except the black smoke that wells into the air from the chimneys of his palace, as his "junk," the sledge amongst it, is consigned to the flames. Of the people who linger within his power, Bernstein alone remains a faithful apostle. Leland denies him, as Peter denied Christ. Bazin maintains that Kane is at last revenged on his parents and on Thatcher "by playing with his social power like a huge toboggan, so as to thrill himself with the dizziness of fortune, or by hitting those who dare to cast aspersion on the moral basis of his actions and his pleasure." [4] His obsessions are hinted at in the final lines of *The Lady from Shanghai*—"She was dead and now I had to try and forget her . . . innocent or guilty, that means nothing, the main thing is to know how to grow up."

The problem of "Rosebud" deserves some attention. Welles himself is the first to admit that "It's a gimmick, really, and rather dollarbook Freud." [5] And as Thompson says resignedly at the end of the film, "I don't think the word 'Rosebud' could explain any man's life. I guess 'Rosebud' is just a piece in the jigsaw puzzle." The sledge is not so precious in itself to Kane (one never sees him look at it, even though it lies amid his belongings at Xanadu) but it conjures up for him memories of a childhood innocence far removed from the "Chicago, New York, and Washington" to which he was so brusquely introduced by Thatcher. The scene in the paperweight that he finds in Susan's room in Xanadu and keeps close to him until his death is of a cottage in a snowstorm, strikingly similar to the lodging house of Mrs. Kane. "The three clues to 'Rosebud' appear at times when Kane is being treated most remotely—in the cryptic death scene in the beginning, in the unfriendly memoirs of his banker guardian, and in the final flashback narration of a cynical butler. The narrations of his closest acquaintances yield no clues to the symbolic truth of his life." [6] Welles's most overt emphasis on the sentimental importance of "Rosebud" is in his three lap-dissolves, showing the abandoned sledge being gradually covered by a snowfall after the young Kane has left with Mr. Thatcher. Just how the sledge eventually reached Xanadu is not explained, although one may conjecture from Kane's first conversation with Susan Alexander, that he rescued it with his mother's belongings "in a warehouse out West."

Negatively, because Rosebud does *not*, as one would expect (and as even Bernstein expects) turn out to be the name of a girl, it stands

---

[4] Ibid.
[5] Dilys Powell, "The Life and Opinions of Orson Welles," *The Sunday Times* (London), February 3, 1963.
[6] Andrew Sarris, "*Citizen Kane*: The American Baroque," *Film Culture*, II (November 1956). [Reprinted in this volume, pp. 102–8.]

as a token of Kane's unhappy relations with people in general. He has no friends, only acquaintances, because he insists on setting himself on a pedestal above those who seek to know him. Arrogance and lack of moral respect are the vices that lead to his isolation. Thompson, in his second interview with Susan at El Rancho, observes: "All the same you know, I can't help being a little sorry for Mr. Kane," to which Susan replies without a moment's hesitation, "Don't you think I am?" It is of course partly due to Welles's own rather sympathetic performance that one feels a measure of pity for this magnate who strives so hard to overcome his fundamental lack of spiritual fibre. Is there, in effect, a sound case to be argued for Kane? Susan's charge—that he made her into an opera singer against her will—is quite patently unfair, especially as in her first meeting with him she admitted that she had always longed to be a singer (although of course this is recalled by Leland, and is therefore suspect because presumably Leland heard only Kane's version of the encounter). Leland himself, though outwardly an endearing personality, is surely ungrateful to Kane when one considers Bernstein's remark that he was the son of a man whose debts at his death were immense. Raymond, with his transparent lust for money (he asks Thompson for a thousand dollars in exchange for information about "Rosebud") is quickly revealed as no more than a parasite on the aging Kane. And Thatcher's testament is of purely biographical interest, its irascible attacks on his *protégé* consisting of part jealousy, part disgust, and part hypocrisy. When all is considered, the two unforgivable sins (in the eyes of the world) committed by Charles Foster Kane are his neglect of the perfectly harmless Emily, his first wife, and his overriding egotism, which ruins the lives of so many, even if some of them almost ask to be maneuvered by his fancy. His insatiable desire for material wealth also condemns him in the opinion of society; but the point to be stressed here is surely that Kane at least *spent* his money, spent it moreover on works of art that endure in fossilized solitude rather than on sensuous pleasures: indeed, the actual comforts of Xanadu seem Spartan in the extreme, and the massive picnic at the end seems rather inappropriate as a result. In the final analysis, no one can deny that Kane earned every ounce of his fortune through his own labor and enthusiasm. He was never one to live on his interest.

Citizen Kane was made in the early autumn of 1940, and it took Welles nine months, working six days a week, to edit. Earlier, he had studied the more important films in cinema history at the Museum of Modern Art. "John Ford was my teacher. My own style has nothing to do with his, but *Stagecoach* was my movie textbook. I ran it over forty times." [7] Then, just prior to shooting the film, he spent several weeks on the sets, making himself familiar with the routine and the equipment. He refused to listen to technicians who told him that what he wanted to do was impossible.

Almost more space has been devoted by critics to the outcry caused by *Citizen Kane* at the time of its opening than to its cinematic merits. However, a short account of events may help to place the film in its historical context. The trouble began when word reached William Randolph Hearst that Welles's film was a caricature of his life. Hearst was a newspaper tycoon like Kane, and the resemblance between the two men appeared to extend even to small details. Susan Alexander was immediately said to correspond to Marion Davies, a starlet with whom Hearst had fallen in love in 1918, only two years after Kane had supposedly met Susan. Hearst offered RKO the $800,000 the film had cost to make if only they would burn it before it was released. When this move failed, he threatened to attack the entire American film industry in his press. RKO encountered difficulty in obtaining circuit bookings for the film as Warners, Loews, and Paramount all relied heavily on the Hearst papers for advertising outlets. Eventually RKO exhibited *Citizen Kane* solely in their own cinemas, and in New York and Los Angeles independent halls had to be hired. Hearst banned his papers from mentioning any RKO films as a result. The scheduled opening was originally February 14, 1941, but the violent clash between Hearst and the production company delayed the first public screening until April 9, 1941 (although the press saw the film privately during March). To this day Welles studiously denies that he modelled Kane on Hearst ("Kane would have liked to see a film of his life, but not Hearst—he didn't have quite enough style"). The film could equally have been based on the life of Jules Brulatour, the owner of Kodak, who wanted to make his wife an important singer.

Citizen Kane is of primary importance in the history of the cinema because of the audacity and virtuosity of Welles's technique, and because of the influence that the style was to exert on films in all parts of the world for the next two decades. It can now be regarded as a clear fifteen years ahead of is time, and even then does not fit into any pattern of aesthetic progress. It remains, like some of Welles's other work, a creation fantastic and unique, a breathtaking reflection of the genius of its inventor. Critics have tried to pin down its significance by drawing literary and dramatic parallels: "For the first time on the screen we have seen the equivalent of a novel by Dos Passos" [8] and

---

[7] Powell, "The Life and Opinions of Orson Welles."
[8] Bazin, *Orson Welles*.

"Apart from its cinematic importance, *Citizen Kane* constitutes, from the point of view of construction, a revolution such as dramatic art has scarcely undergone since Aeschylus" [9] and, more lucid, Dilys Powell's review when the film first came to England in 1941, "There is no question here of experiment for experiment's sake; it is a question of a man with a problem of narrative to solve, using lighting, setting, sound, camera angles, and movement much as a genuine writer uses words, phrases, cadences, rhythms: using them with the ease and boldness and resource of one who controls and is not controlled by his medium."

Yet many of the technical devices used so successfully by Welles had been introduced prior to 1940. His brilliance stems from his ability to synthesize and harmonize all possible stylistic methods into a coherent instrument for telling his story. Only Gregg Toland, the lighting cameraman, agreed with Welles in adopting deep-focus photography and covered sets, and was rewarded with a credit equal in size to that of the director himself on the finished film. Toland was born in Illinois in 1904, worked a great deal with Wyler and, on his death in 1948, was the highest-paid cameraman in Hollywood. "There's never been anyone else in his class," says Welles today. Each scene in *Citizen Kane* was provided with a ceiling, not partial but complete. "I suppose that closing the top of the set was the real revolution we caused. . . . It's disastrous to let a cameraman light a set without a ceiling—it's artificial." Toland was able to use the "pan-focus" process he had developed for two years. It allowed the camera to record objects at a range of twenty inches or several hundred feet with equal clarity. The lens aperture never opened more than $f5.6$, and the lens itself was specially coated which, together with the use of very fast film stock, enabled Welles to shoot scenes that were very brightly lit.

Deep-focus had been exercised, rather haphazardly, at earlier stages in the history of the cinema. An example is to be found in Griffith's *Musketeers of Pig Alley* where the characters advance towards the camera until those in close-up are in as sharp focus as those still following in the background. But after 1925 the use of panchromatic film stock obliged cameramen to abandon deep-focus lenses in favor of "brighter" lenses; and these, when recording close-ups, tended to make everything in the background misty and out of focus. When the sensitivity of film stock improved during the thirties, Renoir was one of the first directors to see the advantages of deep-focus. Several shots in *Boudu sauvé des Eaux* (1932) and *La Règle du Jeu* (1939) demonstrate this. But Welles, assuming that deep-focus presented no technical

---

[9] Jacques Bourgeois, "Le cinema a la recherche du temps perdu," *La Revue du Cinema* (December 1946).

problems to a lively camera crew, systematically employed the lens with the result that his film achieves very much the field of vision encompassed by the human eye, even to the gigantic close-ups (e.g., the lips of the dying Kane as he mumbles "Rosebud"). In later films, particularly *Touch of Evil* and *The Trial*, he was to use this 18.5-mm. focal length increasingly.

The deep-focus photography throughout *Citizen Kane* is apt to echelon the characters, as it were, showing several actions—several points of interest—simultaneously. I will note five out of several examples of Welles's enrichment of the film in this way. First, when Mrs. Kane is signing the form whereby Thatcher is to be the guardian of the young Kane, Welles places the father at the left of the frame, the mother at the right (in close-up), with Thatcher leaning over her, and, in the background, beyond the window, the boy playing in the snow. This shot is not merely economical, but it also keeps one constantly aware of the person whose future is being discussed and decided. Second, the celebration scene at the offices of *The Inquirer*. Leland and Bernstein are seated at the end of a long table with other members of the newspaper staff ranged along each side. In the background Kane is dancing with a troupe of showgirls. Suddenly he strips off his jacket and tosses it towards the camera into the arms of Leland, who is in close-up at the left of the frame. The flying jacket demonstrates the three-dimensional quality that the deep-focus lens creates, and provides just as much of a visual shock as the objects flung "out of the screen" in the much publicized 3-D films thirteen years later. Third, when Kane finds that the besotted Leland has begun an unfavorable review of Susan's operatic *début,* he types out the remainder of the notice himself. Welles shows Kane at his typewriter in close-up at the left of the frame, and one sees Leland stagger down the length of *The Inquirer* newsroom (in sharp focus) towards his boss. By avoiding a series of direct cuts here, Welles counterpoints and visually extends the lull before the quarrel that seems inevitable between the two men. The sharp, deliberate tapping of Kane's machine on the "foreground" soundtrack, as it were, contrasts appropriately with Leland's voice in the background, and accentuates the spatial relationship.

Fourth, when Susan drugs herself in misery after her disastrous performance at the opera house, Welles conveys the implications and urgency of the situation in one remarkable shot, on three levels: in close-up are the glass and the phial of poison resorted to by Susan; in mid-shot the head of Susan, lying in shadow on the pillow; and in the background the door, beneath which appears a strip of light. All this is given dramatic intensity by the soundtrack, with the labored breathing of Susan, and the thunderous knocking of Kane on the locked door. And lastly, when Susan is practising her singing with Matisti, Welles places the piano in the foreground, with Matisti gesticulating on the left, and Susan singing pathetically on the right. Unseen by them both, Kane enters the vast room by a door in the far background. Caught in clear focus, he watches the abortive lesson; this dramatic irony again arouses a feeling of realistic suspense, for the spectator knows that Kane is about to intervene in his usual domineering manner. He is kept in sharp focus all the time as he advances towards the piano.

André Bazin, who has investigated this aspect of Welles's early work so thoroughly,[10] sees in deep-focus a greater freedom for the spectator, who can choose at any one instant in the same shot the elements that interest him, and he underlines how much events and characters can gain in ambiguity, because the significance of each moment of the action is not arbitrarily stressed. This use of deep-focus is closely allied to Welles's keenness to show how his characters can be influenced by their surroundings. For instance, Kane as a man is dwarfed by the lofty, public hall in which he gives his election speech, but his voice and his promises are magnified and boom out over the soundtrack, creating a sense of bombast and inflated power. Similarly Kane is often viewed from a camera set-up at floor level. The tilt, and the corresponding exaggeration of the human figure, display Kane's dominance over the people in his life. When Leland meets him one night in *The Inquirer* offices, only Kane's trouser leg is seen in close-up at the left of the frame while Leland sways on his feet in the background. And when Kane and Susan have one of their final quarrels, in a tent during the picnic near Xanadu, the camera views him alternately from below (as he listens to Susan's harangue, with the screaming of some outraged woman guest outside the tent providing a subtle aural aside) and from above (as he towers over Susan and tells her that he has only helped her out of love). His shadow obscures her and seemingly overawes her. This preponderance is symbolized most unostensibly of all in Susan's bedroom immediately before she leaves her husband. As she stands talking to Kane in mid-shot, a stuffed doll sits near the camera, in parallel profile of Susan, suggesting the true nature of her position in the eyes of Kane—that of a marionette.

Welles also used two other common cinematic devices, creatively and incisively. The wipe, which is usually so artificial, is ironically suitable for bridging the six episodes in which Welles shows the deterioration of the marriage between Kane and Emily at the breakfast table (Kane becomes gradually more and more morose, and Emily ends by reading *The Chronicle,* archrival of Kane's own newspaper, *The Inquirer*). Then there is one startlingly successful vertical travelling shot, in the opera scene. The camera rests on the figure of Susan, singing in

---

[10] Bazin, *Orson Welles.*

rehearsal on the stage; then it moves slowly upwards and at last reaches the topmost catwalk above the curtains. Two technicians look at each other, and one expresses his disapproval (there is a tribute to this shot in Truffaut's *Tirez sur le Pianiste*, when Fido throws his milk bomb onto the gangsters' car). Thus the fact that Susan has a feeble voice and generates only boredom and disgust in her audience is brought home.

Citizen Kane is also rich in "shock images," none of which are so gratuitous as those sprinkled across Buñuel's work. The opening of the film has a sombre tone as Kane's death is revealed in expressionistic terms, but the fade-out on the lighted window in Xanadu is succeeded abruptly by the strident music of the *News on the March* credit card. Thus, within a few minutes of the start of the film, Welles has shown both the distorted, brooding image of Kane's existence, and the brash, realistic version known to the public. Another jolting cut is from Raymond's saying "Like the time his wife left him . . ." to a close-up of a screeching white parakeet behind which, on the verandah of Xanadu, Susan walks away in high dudgeon. This visual shock represents the mental shock sustained by Kane when he realizes Susan has gone, and explains his violent wrecking of her room. It is as though he has suffered a heart attack.

The technical grammar of the film is so richly condensed that a complete exegesis would take up more space than is possible here. No study of *Citizen Kane* would, however, be complete, without mention of Welles's fondness for dissolves and "lightning mixes" (scenes linked by the soundtrack but not by the images). The dissolves are immediately in evidence when at the start of the film the camera crawls up from the "No Trespassing" sign and the wire fences dissolve into heavy gates, then into a series of views, in closer and closer proximity to the palace, with—successively—a cage of monkeys, gondolas, a ghostly, oriental pavilion, an abandoned golf course marker, and an open-air swimming pool in the foreground. These quick shots, merging one with another, convey the remote, portentous power with which Kane has hedged himself in during his life at Xanadu. The "lightning mixes" are more plentiful and rather more difficult to catalogue. Two of the most striking instances are (1) when, during Thatcher's recollections, the shot changes from his wishing the young Kane "a merry Christmas —" to the same man, somewhat older, continuing the sentence "—and a prosperous New Year" just before his *protégé*'s twenty-fifth birthday; and (2) when Kane's clapping at Susan Alexander's piano recital in her own parlor is dovetailed with the applause from a small crowd as Leland campaigns for Kane to be Governor in the 1916 elections, and then almost immediately afterwards Leland's sentence "—who entered upon this campaign . . ." is replaced by that of Kane himself (a second later) in the huge assembly hall, ". . . with one purpose only."

This dramatic continuity illustrates Kane's frightening rise to power.

But *Citizen Kane* is important for its basic construction as well as for the myriad details that comprise its style. Flashbacks were used often before 1940—perhaps Carné's *Le Jour Se Lève* explored their advantages most thoroughly—but Welles was the first director to use them not merely at random but so as to present five biased views of one person. The memories of Thatcher, Bernstein, Leland, Susan, and Raymond, while carefully arranged in chronological order, are all slightly prejudiced. "Each major flashback begins at a later point in time than its predecessor, but each flashback overlaps with at least one of the others, so that the same event or period is seen from two or three points of view." [11] For instance, Susan's *début* in *Salammbo* at the Chicago Opera House is seen three times altogether in the film, in the newsreel, in Leland's flashback when it is seen at rehearsal through his bored eyes in the dress-circle, and in Susan's own memories when the audience is seen as a black, hostile void beyond the glaring footlights. This gives the episode an additional narrative dimension, which is reflected spatially in the lighting and camerawork.

Moreover, these recollections are not marred by the customary aura of age and remoteness, because Welles has so cunningly summarized the key facts of Kane's life in the newsreel. Several of the incidents covered by the *News on the March* bulletin are made to look graining and shaky, as though drawn from some archive, and yet later in the film the *same* shots appear in the course of the flashbacks in crystal *clear* vision. Thus Welles causes events literally to come to life in the flashbacks (the shot of Susan and Kane climbing into a carriage after their wedding, for example). Welles himself recalls that when the film opened in Italy just after the war, a lot of people booed and hissed and even shook their fists at the projection box because they thought the newsreel material was sheer bad photography. The newsreel has a further significance in that it provides a salient outline of Kane's life and enables Welles to dispense with a strictly logical narrative style.

The form of *Citizen Kane*, superficially so diffuse, is in reality highly disciplined. Practically every movement has its complement at another point in the film. Apart from the opening and closing scenes, when the camera begins and ends by focusing in close-up on the "No Trespassing" sign outside Xanadu, one can quote the crane shot that climbs up, over the roof, and down through the skylight of the El Rancho nightclub in Atlantic City. When Thompson first arrives, the neon sign "Susan Alexander-Cabaret" is flashing; when he returns much later in the film and much later in time, the sign is out, signifying the decline of Susan's fortunes since Kane's death. A French critic has

---

[11] Sarris, "*Citizen Kane*: The American Baroque."

noted that the shot is also "the physical image of that violation of consciences and intimacy that the press has perpetrated and that *Citizen Kane* seeks both to represent and to attack." [12]

Nearly all the players in *Citizen Kane* were unknown when the film appeared. Oddly, few of them have established a major reputation over the years. Joseph Cotten still plays the occasional role . . . ; Agnes Moorehead and Everett Sloane also appear in minor parts, though always with distinction, and Erskine Sanford (Carter in this film) was seen to rather better effect as the judge in *The Lady from Shanghai*. Nearly all these actors and actresses had worked with Welles in his Mercury Theatre group, and the performances in *Citizen Kane* are as near perfect as can be. Welles himself has never had a role since that suits his capacity as well as Kane. His first appearance, brash in braces and open-necked shirt, and swinging on his chair as he simultaneously lights his pipe and rebuffs the protests of Walter Thatcher, oozes the almost pardonable arrogance that is the making of Kane's career. Never once does Welles dispel the magnetic aura that Kane seems to carry about with him, even in old age (the makeup staff of RKO succeeded remarkably in making the 25-year-old Welles look at least sixty in some sequences). He has that supremely self-confident air of one who knows in advance precisely what his detractors will say and disarms them with a single witticism or command.

Citizen Kane remains Welles's finest film, a treasury of cinematic metaphors and devices, and a portrait of an incredibly powerful personality. The theme of the life of a grandiose figure ending in tragedy is the blueprint for nearly all Welles's subsequent work (*The Stranger, The Lady from Shanghai, Macbeth, Othello, Confidential Report, Touch of Evil*). Irrespective of the fluctuations of critical opinion (and in the 1962 *Sight and Sound* poll it emerged as the film cited most by critics asked to list the ten best films ever made), it will remain one of the few films of which the long-term influence on the history of the cinema was as remarkable as its initial impact.

[12] "Orson Welles, l'ethique et l'esthetique," *Etudes Cinematographiques*, Nos. 24–25 (1963). (Special issues with contributions by various authors.)

CITIZEN KANE Revisited
by ARTHUR KNIGHT

When in 1952 the British film magazine *Sight and Sound* published the results of an international poll to discover "the ten best films of all time," Orson Welles's *Citizen Kane* fell just short of the magic number, tying with Jean Renoir's *La Grande Illusion* and John Ford's *The Grapes of Wrath* for the eleventh position. In a similar poll ten years later sent to substantially the same group of film critics and historians, *Citizen Kane* was the clear-cut victor—"the best film of all time," if one were to read such listings literally.

What the perspective of an intervening decade had clarified was the fact that *Kane* was indeed a seminal film or, as *Time* magazine might put it, a "watershed" film. When it first appeared, in 1941, most critics busied themselves with pointing out similarities to previous pictures by earlier directors. Welles's technique was described as "eclectic," and the whole thing regarded as a spectacular, precocious stunt. (Welles, incredibly enough, was only twenty-five when he made it.) As had been the case with *The Cabinet of Dr. Caligari* a mere twenty years earlier, the more serious critics wrote it off as a kind of dead end for movies, a one-time happening that had no broader implications for the medium.

Although 20/20 hindsight now makes it apparent that *Kane* was at least ten years ahead of its time, and possibly more, it is no accident that the charge of eclecticism was levelled against Welles when the picture was released. In preparation for his film, he spent literally hundreds of hours in projection rooms—first in New York's Museum of Modern Art, later on the RKO lot—running off pictures from the past. (John Ford was his particular favorite.) He put himself through the same rigorous course of viewing and re-viewing that the French *auteur* directors found so valuable at their *Cinematheque* in Paris, or that film students in our colleges and universities are being exposed to

"*Citizen Kane Revisited*" by *Arthur Knight. From* Action Magazine *4 (1969): 33–35. Reprinted by permission of* Action Magazine.

today. Welles seemed to sense that just as the abstract expressionist must first master the basics of composition and perspective, or a serial composer learns harmony and counterpoint before practicing the more advanced forms of his art, so should the filmmaker be acquainted with all that had gone before—if only to avoid repeating mistakes.

What too many critics overlooked at the time was that, in addition to those techniques and devices that Welles's acquisitive eye picked up during some six months of intensive screenings, he also brought to the medium an unprecedented awareness of the potency of sound. Throughout the thirties, the infant talkies were still learning how to talk. By the time that Welles entered upon the Hollywood scene, at the very end of 1939, the photographed play had become pretty much a thing of the past. Dialogue had grown more naturalistic, acting more intimate; the camera had regained much of its former mobility. But the sound track, with notably few exceptions, merely reproduced dialogue, natural sounds, and music (generally of the "Mickey Mouse" genre). Welles proceeded to change all this.

What is often forgotten about Welles is that his extraordinary career in the thirties embraced not only some of the most exciting theatre of the decade—his all-Negro *Macbeth* in a Haitian setting, his modern-dress *Julius Caesar,* his production of Marc Blitzstein's jazz opera, *The Cradle Will Rock*—but also intensive work in radio. Both of these involved a highly creative use of sound. No one who ever saw his *Macbeth* will forget the rhythmic pounding of jungle drums as an underscore to the mounting tragedy. No one who ever heard his famous *War of the Worlds* on radio will forget the adroit cut-aways from a dreary dance band in a New York hotel to the terse announcement of inexplicable foreign objects landing near Princeton, New Jersey. Long before he came to films, Welles had mastered the added dimension that sound can bring to visuals.

Citizen Kane is virtually a sound man's manual of areas for his special exploration. The film begins with a long series of lap dissolves as the camera moves closer and closer to the one lighted window in Xanadu, Kane's fortress-like Florida estate. To cement the images together, Bernard Herrmann (Welles's composer from his CBS radio days) threaded a series of chords on mounting figures in the strings—a perfect aural counterpoint to the camera's slow rise from the barred gates to the distant light. Herrmann's music is used effectively to establish period (as in the Gay Nineties *Oh, Mr. Kane!* number); but more often Welles borrowed from radio the technique of introducing music in the middle of a scene, then allowing it subtly to change the mood in anticipation of the scene that follows. These musical bridges, unique at the time, have since become a standard technique for all film composers.

But if Welles inspired a new direction for film music, he was even more original in his manipulations of the sound track. His radio training, for example, made him particularly aware of the timbres of voices—their hollow, reverberating sound in a cavernous room (such as the Thatcher Memorial Library), the tinny, filtered sound of a voice-over commentator ("News—on the march!"), the echoes of an empty stairwell ("I'm going to send you to Sing Sing, Gettys! To Sing Sing!"). Indeed, the entire newsreel sequence that follows the death of Kane (except when edited out for most television presentations) demonstrates Welles's special awareness of the qualities of sound; it is as if, in addition to tracing Kane's career through the simulated newsreel clips, he was also tracing the advances in sound recording techniques. Another familiar radio device, one that he was to use far more extensively in the subsequent *Magnificent Ambersons,* is the sound montage —a quick series of flashes revealing the thoughts or reactions of several people or an entire group in words and images. The brilliant breakfast sequence, in which the gradual deterioration of a marriage is compressed into less than two minutes of dialogue tied together by swish pans, is perhaps the most notable example of this technique in *Kane.*

Genuine creativity, however, lies less in noting the similarities between two media than in observing their differences, and in turning these to an advantage. In both radio and the theatre, for example, it is quite impossible to have two or more conversations going on simultaneously. One must see or hear (or both) the sources of the words in order to identify readily each of the speakers. Indeed, one of the theatre's more unpardonable sins is stepping on another's lines. And yet in normal conversation, as Welles clearly understood, we do precisely that most of the time. One seldom waits until a friend has completed a statement before making a response. One never waits until a room is utterly quiet before offering an observation. Voices mount over voices to create tapestries of sound. With uncanny insight, Welles realized that not only can the camera isolate out each of the speakers in a Babel of conversation, but also that the re-recording panel provides complete control over each channel of voices. Thus, he could mix, blend, and balance the dialogue tracks in a completely naturalistic way and still not lose those words or sentences that he considered particularly significant. Such sequences as the party given to celebrate the victory of *The Inquirer* over *The Chronicle* or, late in the film, the lawn *fête* at Xanadu provide multiple illustration of this technique.

Equally adroit and original was Welles's use of dialogue to motivate a cut. Typical is his bridging of several years as banker Thatcher dictates a Christmas letter to the youthful Kane, ending it with "A merry Christmas. . . ." Then, as the voice continues with ". . . and a happy New Year," a jump cut brings us face to face with an older, angrier Thatcher who has lost all taste for his willful, wayward protégé. Overlapping dialogues (accompanying lingering lap dissolves) frequently lead into the various flashback sequences of the film, while sudden stabs of sound—such as the harsh screech of a white cockatoo—vividly punctuate other transitions. Perceptively, the British critic Dilys Powell wrote of *Citizen Kane* in 1941 as the work "of one who controls and is not controlled by his medium." Many of the sound techniques that Welles introduced in this virtuoso first effort still await further exploration by filmmakers today.

More obvious perhaps are the visual innovations of the picture. Contrary to studio practice at the time, Welles felt that all his sets should have ceilings. This not only affected the sound quality, giving it a greater realism, but also afforded him a far wider range of camera angles to shoot from—particularly the low-angle shots he favored because they emphasized the bulk (and the stature) of his hero. While this created lighting problems for his cinematographer, the late, great Gregg Toland, it also encouraged Toland to experiment with new film stocks and, especially, with new lenses. It seems odd today, but during the thirties the standard photography—even for such realistic films as *I Am a Fugitive from a Chain Gang*—called for soft focus and diffused lighting. Toland's wide-angled lenses created a revolution. Not only did the new focal lengths lend depth to sets that were relatively modest, but they kept everything, whether near or far, in needle-sharp focus. (Welles augmented this effect by his extraordinary utilization of split-screen processing in such sequences as Boss Gettys grimly surveying Kane from what seems to be the very top of an enormous convention hall, or when Kane in a large close-up types out his review of his mistress's disastrous operatic debut while a drunken Jed Leland —who should have been writing it—weaves his way down the entire length of the deserted newspaper office.)

Looking back on *Citizen Kane* from the vantage point of more than a quarter of a century, it is astonishing how fresh and original it still appears. The crispness of its black-and-white photography, the rightness of its performances, the intricate interlocking of its multifaceted story have lost none of their fascination. What time has revealed, however, is the very special way that innovative techniques work their way into the fabric of filmmaking in general. Unfortunately, Welles himself was to have shockingly few opportunities to direct again after *Kane* was completed—and never with the freedom or autonomy he enjoyed during the production. But the men who worked with him and were encouraged by him to expand their horizons—men like his coproducer (and cowriter) John Houseman, men like Toland and Herrmann, men like Robert Wise and Mark Robson, who were his editors, not to mention the superb acting company that formed the nucleus of his Mercury

Theatre—they moved on to make films for other directors and other studios. But because their paths had crossed Welles's, because they had worked on *Citizen Kane,* their entire approach to the medium was profoundly changed. And gradually, less by imitation than by inspiration, *Citizen Kane* has altered the look not only of American films, but of films the world over.

COMMENTARIES

CITIZEN KANE
JORGE LUIS BORGES

Citizen Kane (which is called "The Citizen" in Argentina) has at least two themes. The first, of an almost banal foolishness, tries merely to please as entertainment. It accomplishes this end very strikingly: a vain millionaire accumulates statues, gardens, palaces, pools, cars, libraries, men, and women; in the image of a collector of yesteryear . . . , he discovers that such a mixture and such abundance are but vanity and only vanity; at the moment of death he only desires one object in the world: a little sled he loved as a child!

The second theme is far superior. It unites a reference to Koheleth with that of another nihilist, Franz Kafka. The subject, at the same time metaphysical and detective story-like, psychological and allegorical, is the discovery of the secret soul of a man, beyond the works he has constructed, the words he's said, the many destinies he has ruined. The method is that of Joseph Conrad in *Chance* (1914) and that of the great film *The Power and the Glory*: the rhythmic integration of disparate scenes without chronological order. In astonishing and endlessly varied ways, Orson Welles exhibits the fragments of the life of the man, Charles Foster Kane, and invites us to combine and reconstruct them. Shapes of multiplicity and diversity abound in the film: the first scenes show in passing the treasures accumulated by Foster Kane; in one of the last, a poor suffering woman plays on the floor of the palace, which is also a museum, with an enormous crossword puzzle. We understand at the end that the fragments do not have a hidden unity: the unhappy Foster Kane is a shadow, a mere chaos of appearances (a possible deduction, foreseen by Hume, by Ernest Mach, and by our Macedono Fernandez: no man knows who he is, no man is anyone). In one of the tales of Chesterton, *The Head of Caesar*, I believe, the

"Citizen Kane" by Jorge Luis Borges, From Sur *83 (1945). Reprinted by permission of* Sur *and the author. Translated from the French by Mark Bernheim and Ronald Gottesman.*

hero observes that nothing is more frightening than a centreless labyrinth. This film is just that labyrinth.

We all know that a party, a palace, a great enterprise, a writers' and journalists' banquet, a cordial atmosphere of frank and spontaneous friendship, are essentially horrifying. *Citizen Kane* is the first film to portray them with some awareness of this truth. The execution is worthy, in general, of the great theme. The shots have admirable depth, shots whose backgrounds (such as Pre-Raphaelite paintings) are no less faithful and exact than the foregrounds.

I dare predict, however, that *Citizen Kane* will endure in the same way certain films of Griffith or of Pudovkin "endure": no one denies their historic value but no one sees them again. It suffers from grossness, pedantry, dullness. It is not intelligent, it is genial in the sombrest and most germanic sense of the word.

The Originality of Welles as a Director
ANDRÉ BAZIN

Let us study a typical scene of Welles's—the botched poisoning of Susan in *Citizen Kane*. The screen opens on Susan's room seen from behind the nighttable. In the first shot, right up against the camera, an enormous glass holds almost ¼ of the picture, along with a little spoon and an open medicine bottle. The glass hides Susan's bed from us almost entirely, plunging it in an area of shadow from which only some indistinct, raspy sounds escape, as from a drugged sleeper. The room is empty; all the way at the back of this private desert is the door, made to seem even farther away by the false perspective, and behind this door, noises. Without having seen anything but a glass and having heard two noises of different sound levels, we have suddenly understood the situation—Susan has locked herself in the room to take

"The Originality of Welles as a Director" [editor's title] by André Bazin. From Orson Welles *by André Bazin (Paris: Chavane, 1950), pp. 52–55. Reprinted by permission of the publisher. Translated by Mark Bernheim and Ronald Gottesman.*

poison; Kane is trying to enter. The dramatic structure of the scene is essentially based on the distinction between the two sounds: the gasps, nearby, of Susan and the bangings of her husband behind the door. A tension is established between these two poles, held at a distance by the depth of focus. Now the pounding is louder as Kane tries to break down the door with his shoulder; he succeeds. We see him appear in miniscule in the frame of the doorway and hurry towards us. The spark is struck between the two dramatic poles of the image. The scene is finished.

To better understand the originality of this directing, which might appear too natural and easy to achieve its end, we must show what Welles did *not* do. The scene could have been broken down at least into five or six shots: a long shot of the glass and the medicine, a shot of Susan gasping in her sweaty bed (at this moment he knocks at the door), a view of Kane pounding on the door, the creation of suspense by a brief parallel montage (that is, a series of views of inside, then outside the room) until we see the picture of the door yielding to Kane's assault, then Kane's back rushing to the bed perhaps, and finally a close-up shot of Kane bending over Susan.

One clearly sees that the classical sequence consisting of a series of shots analyzing the action according to the meaning the director wishes us to take resolves itself here into a single continuous shot. Moreover, Welles's extreme use of deep focus tends to destroy the notion of the shot as a unity of cutting that one can call the shot-sequence. Paradoxically, the camera's immobility becomes a very complicated movement when the scene itself is in movement.

CITIZEN KANE
FRANÇOIS TRUFFAUT

The appearance of *Citizen Kane* in 1946 was an extraordinary event for cinemaphiles of our generation. After the Liberation, we discov-

"Citizen Kane" by François Truffaut. From L'Express (November 26, 1959). Reprinted by permission of L'Express. Translated by Mark Bernheim and Ronald Gottesman.

ered the American film and did away with, one after the other, all the French directors we had admired, for lack of anything better, during the war. Even stronger was our dissatisfaction with French actors in comparison to Americans. Down with Pierre Fresnay, Jean Marais, Edwige Feuillere, Raimu, Michele Morgan; up with Cary Grant, Humphrey Bogart, James Stewart, Gary Cooper, Lauren Bacall, Gene Tierney, Ida Lupino, Edward G. Robinson.

We liked everything, provided it was from Hollywood, and we wolfed down as many originals as copies. We lived them up to the point of exact copying of dubbing—what a perversion—and at any point when I arrived in the middle of a thriller, I could tell if the French voice of Bogart was Claude Peran's or Raymond Loyer's. And at night, in my sleep, I forced myself to hear again the inflections of the warm and modulated voice of Claire Guibert, heard 100 times behind the figures of Lauren Bacall, Ingrid Bergman, Ida Lupino, and so many others.

It is *Citizen Kane*, which never existed as vin ordinaire, which sobered us and made of us demanding cinemaphiles. This film, I believe, consecrated a great many of us to the vocation of cinéaste.

It was shown regularly for five or six years and we went to see it at each showing—first at Marbeuf, it went then to L'Artistic, to Reflets, to Studio Raspail, to Studio Parnasse, and finally to Cine-Opera which became the Vendome, where it is shown again today. Despite its very bad subtitling (always the same, alas!), *Citizen Kane*, no doubt by the richness of its sound track, made us finally disgusted with dubbing.

We loved this film because it was complete: psychological, social, poetic, dramatic, comic, baroque, strict, and demanding. It is a demonstration of the force of power and an attack on the force of power, it is a hymn to youth and a meditation on old age, an essay on the vanity of all material ambition and at the same time a poem on old age and the solitude of exceptional human beings, genius or monster or monstrous genius.

A Mad Gamble

It is at the same time a "first" film by virtue of its quality of catch-all experimentation and a "last" film by its comprehensive picture of the world. I only understand today, thirteen years after the great shock of July 1946, why *Citizen Kane* is the film it is and in what it is unique; it is the only "first" film directed by a famous man.

Chaplin was only a little refugee mime when he began; Renoir was, in the eyes of the profession, only his father's son playing as an amateur with film and spending his family's money (nothing new, then, in Landerneau). Hitchcock was only a designer of credits who rose in esteem when he directed *Blackmail*. Orson Welles, however, was known to all America and not only for his broadcast on the Martians. He was a famous man whose shooting one awaited ("Silence, a genius is shooting," cracked the newpapers) so avidly that he was forced to make not a film which permitted him to get started in the industry, but THE film, the one which sums up and prefigures all the others. And, my God, this mad gamble was very nearly won.

My feelings as a spectator in 1959 reviewing *Citizen Kane*? No problem, as the saying goes; but I have the feeling that if I were at least ten years old and a cinemaphile who had waited years to see this film of which everyone speaks in film histories, I would be cruelly disappointed.

Citizen Kane is classed among the ten best films in the world and naturally I don't agree. First because my list changes each year in response to the new films and re-viewings of old ones, and especially because I am not concerned with the historical importance of films. To *Citizen Kane* I prefer *Othello,* even *M. Arkadin, Ambersons,* and maybe even *The Lady from Shanghai*.

Orson Welles is certainly of the ten greatest cinéastes in the world; one can question his talent, but not his genius. ("Orson Welles is a genius without talent," says *The New Yorker*.) To shoot *Citizen Kane* at twenty-five years of age, is this not the dream of all the young habitués of the cinematheques?

Orson Welles was a radio man, a journalist, and a man of the theatre. Aside from the miracle of genius, there is nothing miraculous in *Citizen Kane*; this film reveals effectively, if viewed reasonably, the qualities of a man of radio, journalism, and theatre.

In re-viewing it, I noticed that I knew it by heart, but like a record rather than a film; I wasn't always certain of the image which was going to follow, but I was sure of the sound which was coming, of the quality of voice of whoever was going to speak, of the musical linking which led to the next sequence.

If *Chin Chin* is the only play in Paris which has an auditory value, then Billetdoux is the only playwright who comes, like Orson Welles, from radio, and that is why we know the value of one accent opposed to another, of musical concatenation, and his play, like Welles's movie, evokes, by its aural richness, a "radiophonique" film.

A JOURNALIST'S FILM

I like the differentiation formulated by Nabokov in his interviews between "journalists" (like Hemingway) and "artists" (like Proust).

In this respect, *Citizen Kane* is primarily the film of a journalist and one can speak of a "page setting" as well as a stage setting. Half the scenes are faked in this film, which becomes almost an example of animation because of the film trickery. How many shots based on the depth of field are obtained by the trick of "mask against mask," which is the cinemagraphic equivalent of fake picture arrangement practiced in tabloids? The last films of Hitchcock, for example, make great use of trickery, but the tricks are almost invisible since they are aimed to reinforce the realism.

Citizen Kane is thus a journalist's film in comparison to the following; *The Magnificent Ambersons* is an artist's film—one which is moreover directed in constant opposition to *Citizen Kane*: long scenes, primarily of the actor before the camera, dilatation of real time, etc.

If *Citizen Kane* has aged, it is in its experimental aspects. Everything happens as if Orson Welles, in his fabled pride, had rejected the rules of film and its optical limits, and as if, by tricks, more astute and successful than anyone else's, he made his film resemble plastically the American cartoons where the imagination of the artist allows him to place a person in full view, men behind him, the speaker in full length portrait, and at the back of the drawing, thirty people whose neckties are drawn as clearly as the wart on the nose of the main subject in the cartoon. It is this miracle, unique, never repeated, which is accomplished before us fifty times in a row in *Kane*.

An Invented Moral

Another surprise: this film which appeared crazed with luxury and riches seems to us today to have been made on a shoestring and with literally trifles. There are many stock shots, many big pieces of furniture, many walls designed with optical illusions, and especially many close-up scenes of bells, of cymbals, of newspapers, many fade-outs. But even this mystification is turned to advantage by the prodigy of Kenosha. We know too many European or American films which cost fortunes yet seem skimpy.

That which is found in *Kane* already, but which is rediscovered better expressed in the rest of his work, is a world view at the same time very personal, very generous, and very noble. There is no vulgarity, no meanness in this satiric film; an invented and inventive moral, antibourgeois and anticonventional; a standard of behavior, of things to do and not to do.

We must be able to contrast, in this study, the sedentary cineastes and the traveling cineástes. The former film stories are only able with great difficulty, towards the end of their careers, to pass from particular ideas to general ones. The latter, little by little, insensibly are able to film the world. Because of the social conditions which keep them sedentary, critics, whether they be literary or film, are always insensitive to the greatest beauties of the films of Renoir, Rossellini, Hitchcock, and Welles; for these reveal the ideas of itinerant men, emigrés, international observers.

In the greatest films of our time, there is always a scene at an airport (the best one being that in *Confidential Report*); when the plane is full, Mr. Arkadin offers $10,000 to someone for his ticket.

But I'm speaking too much and I had better stop.

The Most Advanced Film Screened in Class This Year: A Catalogue of Effects
MICHAEL STEPHANICK

Orson Welles's *Citizen Kane* is the most advanced film seen by Film Production students thus far because of its rich experimentation, innovations, and combinations in photography, editing, and sound. The success of the film, however, does not rest alone on Welles's diverse and sophisticated use of editing, sound, and lights. It is his careful planning and coordination of techniques which allows the smooth transitions which are the foundation of *Kane*. With excellent direction, *Kane* becomes a landmark for its total stimulation of the intellect and emotions.

Undoubtedly the most important aspect of the film is Welles's treatment of time and its transitions. In order to discuss my appreciation for this film, I must comment about specific techniques.

First, Welles used objects to suggest enormous proportions relevant

"The Most Advanced Film Screened in Class This Year: A Catalogue of Effects" by Michael Stephanick. From Montage 3 (1970): 5-7. Reprinted by permission of the author and the Center for Film Production.

to the basis of Kane's life. These include the shots of Xanadu at the opening, Thatcher's statue and library, Kane's "Declaration of Principles," the letters of the *Inquirer* building by the windows, the large poster of Kane at the rally, Kane's typing of the word "weak" in Leland's review, Susan's unflattering review scattered on the floor (reminiscent of Kane's "Declaration of Principles" which Leland sends him in that same scene), the area shot of Xanadu (showing the staircase, statues, fireplace), the long series of arches in the house, and the mass of "junk" (including the Rosebud sleigh) covering the floor. Welles uses objects to suggest symbolism with a shocking effect—the bright light burning out to signify the virtual end of Susan's unproductive singing career, and the screaming bird to emphasize the shock sustained by Kane when he realizes that Susan had actually left him.

In his deployment of lighting, he again uses two types to heighten the dramatic effect. I would call one the "quick cut" of lights used in the beginning at Xanadu when Kane dies, the light from the projector going out after the newsreel, the flash of lightning over the "El Rancho" nightclub, the harsh opening of stage lights at Susan's debut, and the quick change from dark to light and back to dark again as Kane walks through the arches at Xanadu. The second type consists of diverse angle lighting, including the light beams coming through the openings in the projection room, the ghoulish effect caused by the low lighting of the nightclub, the skylights in the Thatcher Library (almost producing a spotlight effect), the gaslights shining up and out, the side lighting in the *Inquirer* office after the election casting long shadows, the light from the bay window which divides Susan's face while on her recovery bed, and the selective top lighting which gave a "museum" effect to Xanadu when Thompson was talking to the butler.

Welles showed a fondness for deep shadows and silhouettes. As for deep shadows, we find examples with Kane just before he dies, the projection-room sequence, Kane's long shadow when searching for the drunk Leland, Kane's foreboding shadow over Susan after the show, the "rooster" Kane projects on the wall, and Kane's shadow as he walks down the stairs in Xanadu. Silhouettes consisted of Kane dead on his bed, the men filing past the screen, and Kane's top hat in front of Leland's office door (which followed through very nicely from one end of the office to the other). What I term as "selective shadowing" refers to the times when those talking are in shadows or darkness. This allows for quick repetition of lives or concentration on one character. (Welles further diversifies this technique by putting the person being discussed in the shadow.) The best examples of this: the projection room (and the same people at the end in Xanadu), Kane's "Declaration" from the darkness, the rally where only Leland can be distinguished in the crowd, Kane and Gettys (Ray Collins) in alternate shadows arguing in Susan's apartment, and (quite exclusively) Kane sitting in the box at the opera with his wildly shifting eyes the only things visible on an otherwise (shadow-) masked face.

His scenes using mirrors and reflections were subdued but complementary. Mirrors are used twice; first in Susan's apartment (nicely complementing the framed pictures), and second the multi-imaged Kane, his newly smashed life passing down the corridor in silence. Reflections are noted with Bernstein's (Everett Sloane) image on the desk top and the dancing Kane in the office window.

With his training in radio, Welles had no trouble producing dramatic backgrounds and quick cuts with his sound editing. The booming of the newsreel jolts one from the sedate (deathbed) to a fabricated image of Kane (amplified by the demonstrator in the newsreel with the bullhorn); the crack of thunder which leads to the low-keyed nightclub music; the echoes within the library and hollow sound of the closing vault and door; Kane's party, with the singing and the marching band (showing a noticeable drum beat, comparable to that of the blues singer at the picnic); Kane's booming voice at the rally; the door closing from Susan's flat, which cuts off Kane's voice and substitutes traffic (quite a demeaning transition); Kane's singular clapping during the opera; and the rapping of the typewriter, the wrecking of Susan's room (especially glass objects), and the butler's voice echoing through the now empty Xanadu.

Depth was much easier to obtain with the full ceilings used to give reinforcement to any implications of size or scope which Welles wished to make. The very low angle shot of Kane after dropping the paperweight and the nurse's elongated shadows make the room appear extra large (this scene seemed to have been shot through a concave lens apparatus of some sort); the long tracking shot over the rooftops down into the "El Rancho" nightclub (similarly used at the end with the long shot of Kane's "junk" ending with "Rosebud"); the construction of the *Inquirer* building, with its poles, beams, guard rails, and lights, which was geometrically perfect; Leland at the hospital (soft focus giving a feeling of deterioration); Gettys surveying the campaign from far above (even dwarfing Kane's poster); Gettys walking down the stairway (using the spiral construction to complement the reverse cutting); after Susan's suicide attempt; glass and poison (large) in half-light of foreground, Susan in shadows of the middle ground, Kane silhouetted by the doorway in the background; and Susan's walk through the multiple archways at Xanadu. Each time Welles used deep focus (seven times, I believe; the nightclub, library, boarding house, Kane's party, Kane typing, singing lesson, and the aging Kane at Xanadu). He not only allows the audience selection of attention; he goes further to work in framing, lighting, shadows, and silhouettes.

Probably the most important aspect of the film was, as mentioned before, his transition and treatment of time. Welles uses every technique possible to obtain smooth transitions. (These "smooth" transitions may call for a jolt now and then to pull the audience through time; the professional treatment of the change overrides the jump and it is hardly noticed.) It begins with the long tracking shot to Xanadu, from the "No Trespassing" sign to the house. The next was from the projection room to the thunderstorm. Twice he employs a triple transition successfully.

The first was the snow-covered "Rosebud" to the new metal sled from Thatcher ("Merry Christmas") ending with "And A Happy New Year" about fifteen years later. The second was the time Kane was sitting in the parlor listening to Susan sing; his clapping for her performance led to the applause of a crowd hearing Leland campaigning for Kane. The speech Leland makes is finished by Kane himself at the huge hall (effective transition in size of audience and area of performance). Two transitions deal with pictures: the staff photograph in the *Chronicle* window to the actual men at the party and the address number "185" (Susan's apartment) to the photograph on the front page of the newspaper (each opposite of the other). The breakfast sequence succeeded because we knew the time lapses were coming. Thus, each drastic change was accepted and appreciated (change in clothing, temperament, length and tone of conversation, ending with silence at the long table). As soon as we see Bernstein lift the headline proof ("Fraud At the Polls"), it is lowered to reveal a disgusted Leland, who throws the paper to the street. (The street is cobblestone. Kane meets Susan on a cobblestoned street. His political future and marriage end on cobblestones.)

The screaming bird, although a pleasant diversification, is one of those shock cuts which works only because of Welles's quick implementation of depth (arches) and lighting (shadows). In my opinion, the best transition took place when Kane was finishing Leland's notice. I refer specifically to the composition of the frame. Kane takes up about one eighth in the upper right-hand corner (cut diagonally); the rest of the press room is in darkness. As Leland finishes his review, what was once Kane now becomes structural shadows. What was once darkness becomes the aged Leland. This particular scene (keeping its perfect symmetry) not only bridges time and point of view well; it also gives one the feeling that Leland's memories are once again fading back into the shadows of his past life.

Although my own reactions to *Citizen Kane* were very favorable, writing this paper was quite difficult. It seems that the difficulty stemmed from the inherent "completeness" of *Kane*; completeness in the context of each foot of film complementing, enhancing, linking the other to form a total film . . . THE example of the potentials of film. As soon as I tried to classify *Kane* down into small subdivisions (lighting, sound, photography), I realized that what I had was literally hundreds of specific points. After assembling these points for review, all I had left was a helter-skelter composition; reinforcing my belief that *Citizen Kane* should be reviewed from an overall viewpoint . . . it seems that this is one film which defies "final and definitive analyzing."

Personally, I think that *Citizen Kane* is undoubtedly the finest film we have screened this year. Probably it is the most important film I have ever seen. Besides being technically perfect, the general story outline and acting made it quite an enjoyable and stimulating film. Much more important than my accolades is the feeling that this is the first film that I have learned anything from. For me, this is the only time the film appreciation aspects of the Film Production course has had any direct relation to that of filmmaking. This realization that the two have begun to mesh together is probably a reflection on the genius of Orson Welles's direction.

From *The Films of Orson Welles*
CHARLES HIGHAM

CHARLES FOSTER KANE AND WILLIAM RANDOLPH HEARST
COMPARED AND CONTRASTED

One crucial question we must ask ourselves about *Kane* is: does the film accurately reflect William Randolph Hearst's life? Welles has in recent years continued to insist that Kane was not Hearst. He told the *New York Herald Tribune* (September 11, 1951):

> *From* The Films of Orson Welles *by Charles Higham (Berkeley: The University of California Press, 1970) pp. 21–24, 45–47. Copyright © 1970 by the Regents of the University of California. Reprinted by permission of the Regents. Headings supplied.*

He was a great figure. I didn't have a battle with him. He had one with me. *Citizen Kane* was *not* an exposé of Hearst as everyone believes. I didn't make a picture about him.

Hearst was raised by his mother. He had a very happy childhood. My man Kane was raised by a bank. That's the whole point of the picture. They were different types of men. For example, my man Kane would never have fought me the way Hearst did. Instead, he would probably have offered me a job.

Hearst and the people around him did me terrible harm after the picture appeared. Some day when I write my autobiography I'll tell of the damage that they did me, and the frame-ups they tried.

The big similarity between Hearst and Kane is that both of them had no responsibility to the people. But in spite of everything I hold no malice toward him. I don't see why anyone should hold any malice toward him.

We must admit, first, that the portrait is a caricature, and that the picture of Hearst's relationship with his mistress, Marion Davies, is not intended to be literal: her devotion to Hearst was absolute, and his death came to her as a bitter blow.[1] The real Hearst was capable of love, and life at San Simeon, his fabled ranch in California, sparkled in its heyday with a brightness and gaiety contradictory to the squalid luxury of Kane's ranch picnic and the echoing, tomblike emptiness of Xanadu.

In other respects, the film follows Hearst's career with mixed fidelity. The plot adjustments are significant. Both Hearst and Kane were only children, born in 1863, and both were expelled from Harvard. Hearst's father and mother were not, like Kane's, poverty-stricken boardinghouse keepers. George Hearst was a well-to-do farmer's son, whose silver strike at the Comstock Lode made him a millionaire, and whose later interest in the Homestake Mine still further increased his massive fortune; he became a senator and earned a respected place in the American Dictionary of Biography. In the film these parents are left a deed to the Colorado Lode by a defaulting boarder, Fred Grange, and the Kane fortune is thus founded not by the acumen and push of a paternal figure but by blind chance.

Hearst's love for his mother is echoed in Kane's love for his, and the Rosebud image—symbol of a lost childhood and the protection of

---

[1] Others have taken a grimmer view, hinting at homosexuality and other perversions and suggesting that Marion Davies was often kept a virtual prisoner at San Simeon. We will probably never know the truth, but I have preferred the more charitable view.

a mother—is an apt reflection of the fact that Hearst was forever haunted by the memory of the charming, tender, and noble Phoebe Hearst.

The origin of the character of Susan Alexander Kane[2] has usually been attributed to Marion Davies alone, and the portrait is indeed visually based on her: the nervous doll's face, the aureole of blonde hair, the chirrupy voice. It is true, too, that through his Cosmopolitan Pictures outfit, first in New York and then in California, and by purchasing a major shareholding interest in MGM (and later Warner Brothers) Hearst secured for her a career in the cinema which she really didn't want, and was embarrassed to see applauded by every Hearst newspaper critic who valued his job. In fact, a stronger foundation of the character is in Sybil Sanderson, Hearst's first love, an opera singer whose initial American appearance at the Met was applauded in an exorbitantly large article in Hearst's *San Francisco Examiner* (prototype of Kane's *Inquirer*); for her the infatuated Massenet composed *Thaïs* and *Manon*—the mode of the former appropriately and perfectly parodied in Herrmann's *Salammbô* excerpts. Sybil Sanderson died ruined by drink and ill-health in her late thirties, her career dogged by scandals. Although Hearst's wife, Milicent Wilson, was a dancer and not, like Emily Monroe Norton, the niece of the president, much of her personality is echoed in the gentle, staid, and unexciting Emily.

Politically, the parallels with Hearst are often startlingly close, for instance in reference to *The Inquirer* having started the Spanish-American War.

Hearst bought the New York *Morning Journal* in 1895; it was originally an unsuccessful paper, and he changed it into a one-cent sheet of a popular type. He raided the New York *World* for members of Joseph Pulitzer's staff. The combination of sensationalism and jingoism elevated the circulation to 1,506,000 copies. He attacked President McKinley (as Kane attacked President Monroe [sic]), and provoked war with Spain. Later came the Chicago *American*, paralleling the Chicago paper for which Leland worked. During the depression, he sold or scrapped papers, like Kane.

The famous exchange of telegrams between Hearst and Frederic Remington, an artist whom he sent to sketch the Spanish butchery in 1896, is reproduced almost intact in the script. When Remington cabled the *Journal*, "Everything quiet. There is no trouble here. There will be no more. I wish to return." Hearst replied: "Please remain. You furnish the pictures; I'll furnish the war." Later, Hearst published a Remington drawing of a Cuban girl stripped for searching by Cuban

---

[2] Susan Alexander was the name of Welles's screenplay typist.

soldiers; the rival newspaper, the *World,* managed to produce the girl herself, who confessed she had been searched under conditions of privacy by matrons, and that Remington could not have drawn her.

Once the film closely echoes an actual conversation: the remark Kane makes to Walter Parks Thatcher when the banker complains that the newspapers are losing a million dollars a year—"I'll have to close this place—in sixty years." This is directly drawn from Phoebe Hearst's comment upon learning that her son's *Examiner* and *Journal* were losing the same amount: "At that rate, he could last thirty years." Bernstein is based on two of Hearst's associates, Arthur Brisbane and S. S. Carvalho, and Jedediah Leland is based on John Francis Neylan, the Irish lawyer and political reporter who fought gallantly against graft and became Hearst's counsel and lawyer for the Hearst empire: a man of probity, he was often thought of as Hearst's conscience, and he is heartlessly parodied in the figure of the sophomoric, verbose, and often foolish figure presented on the screen.[3] There are parallels, too, in the character of Jim W. Gettys with Boss Charles F. Murphy, a political manipulator who opposed Hearst at the time Hearst ran for governor of New York; Thatcher is a caricature of J. P. Morgan. Kane's politics authentically echo Hearst's: Hearst began as a Jeffersonian democrat, using *The San Francisco Examiner* as a radical organ to fight political corruption, big business, and monopolies, while at the same time deeply involved in business ventures of his own. Later, he became fascist, exploiting a fascist potentiality in the lower middle class, a class that had once been as Jeffersonian as he was.

As Raymond Gram Swing wrote in his *Forerunners of American Fascism*: "During the lifetime and power of this single man, the entire economic fabric was made anew. We see in him the beginning of the modern era, hear through him the social outcry against it, and find him today, no longer a rebel, but resigned to it and accepting its fascist implications."[4] Kane's speeches in the film echo Hearst's, and also Hearst's letters—like the famous one written in 1906 to Arthur Brisbane and quoted by W. A. Swanberg in his definitive *Citizen Hearst*:

> We still maintain a republican form of government, but who has control of the primaries that nominate the candidate? The corporations have. Who control the conventions? The corporations. Who own the bosses and the elected officials? Are they representatives of

---

[3] Leland's dismissal for his unfavorable notice of Susan Kane's operatic debut echoes Hearst's sacking of many for similar "mistakes."
[4] Julian Messner, 1935.

the people or the corporations? . . . If the corporations do all this —and they surely do—can we any longer maintain that this is government for the people?[5]

In his campaign for the governorship of New York, expertly condensed and parodied in the film, Hearst promised "government ownership" to restore to the people "everything the corporations have stolen from them." Later, when Hearst's Americanism—like Kane's—changed its meaning he began to admire Hitler and Mussolini. In the midthirties, after he had established his fascist stand and had visited Hitler, Hearst attacked the communist menace. So the changes were rung and the film mockingly rings them too.

And *Kane*'s final conclusion is the same as Swanberg's, finishing his life of Hearst on a series of question marks. Studying that life, Swanberg wrote, was for most of his contemporaries "as confusing as adding two and two and discovering for once that it did not make four." Swanberg concludes that Hearst would have been dangerous in high office and that his rejection by the voters was a fine proof of the democratic system.

> He had integrity, on occasion. He had principles and beliefs which he firmly swore by at any given time but which could fluctuate as wildly as a compass near the pole. His crippling weakness was instability, vacillation, his inability to anchor his thinking to a few basic, rocklike truths that were immovable in his heart. . . . For all his potency of utterance, he seemed a creature of caprice, lacking real substance.

(In some ways an appropriate comment on the worst side of Welles himself.) Swanberg adds that Hearst was "unrivaled in the magnificence of his failure, the scope of his defeats, the size and scope of his disappointments." The film exactly captures this quality of magnificent catastrophe in a style not dissimilar to that which characterized Hearst's journalism—as Swanberg says, "Combining elements of the peep-show, the Grand Guignol, and the foghorn." Welles's achievement was to blend those elements into art. As Swanberg says: "Who but Citizen Hearst would have set himself up as a king, owned seven castles, fought for the common man, looted the world of art, squired a bevy of actresses through Europe?" The answer is no one. And who but Orson Welles, the explosive *Wunderkind* of American radio, theater, and film, could have brought his life to the screen? No one again. One is left only with the wish that Welles had drawn his own conclusions

[5] New York: Charles Scribner's Sons, 1961.

about this friend of the working man, the Jeffersonian, the fascist, the master of empires, instead of leaving us with an enigma as baffling as a great stone Easter Island face. . . .

CITIZEN KANE: A SUMMARY EVALUATION

From this close analysis of *Citizen Kane*, we can draw certain conclusions. In this great but unequal work, sometimes immature, raw, and rash, at others confident, mature, and spacious, the contrasts are extreme. The lapses are not the least extraordinary things about the film: for example the artistic cheats whereby witnesses to Kane's career describe visually things they cannot possibly have seen. Even if we allow that Kane's descriptions of things that happened could have been echoed by Leland, we cannot accept that Leland would have been able to describe in detail the confrontation between Kane, Mrs. Kane, Susan, and Gettys at which he was not an interloper; nor can we swallow the device whereby Susan is able to describe what Jedediah Leland did with his program in his seat in the stalls, or that Bernstein went to sleep in the balcony.

In his handling of the narrative parts of the film—most notably, the opening and closing passages—Welles's command of visual effect is altogether striking. In his poetic images, such as the recurrent allusions to the snow scene, and the wonderful use of dissolves throughout, he is the complete master. He is weakest when he handles the important dialogue scenes involving Leland and Kane either in a mode of heavy comedy or in showy cadenzas with the camera seemingly lying on the floor. Too often he lets his technique draw attention to itself, permitting us to look at a muslin ceiling (not always convincing anyway) when we would be better engaged in looking into the characters' faces as they emphasize points in a phrase. It is, no doubt, a mark against his technique that one often notes things while listening to the sound track that were altogether lost while watching the film unfold.

How much do we really know about Kane after Thatcher, Bernstein, Leland, Susan, and Raymond have filled in their own sections of the puzzle? First, through the newsreel, we are made aware of Kane's greed, his passion for possessions, and for making the grandiose gesture, symbolized through his construction of Xanadu: the stentorian commentary is in itself a satirical commentary on his ambitions and achievements, and a symbolic representation of Kane's pride.

We learn that, politically, he is a cynic, taking up many political ideas in turn and wringing each dry. This cynicism and opportunism, attractive when seen in opposition to the stiffly correct Thatcher, later look vacuous and futile; *The Inquirer* is simply a tabloid rag posing as a crusading organ, trumpeting its ideals as a prankish circulation stunt. Kane's growing egotism is pointed up by Leland, who also does not miss the tender side of Kane, shown in his feelings for Susan in the early stages. Susan shows us Kane's loneliness and lovelessness, and indeed she sees precisely eye to eye with Leland (who never had much time for her) in noticing that Kane needs love but cannot give it to others.

Kane is a selfish opportunist with delusions of grandeur; yet somehow, and partly through Welles's performance, he emerges as almost altogether likable, even lovable. He has energy, dash, humor, charm; and he shares with the director himself a youthful contempt for the fuddy-duddy, the respectable, the dull. We are made to feel that although *The Inquirer* is worthless as a political organ, it is probably a lively and a first-class newspaper. Kane's furthering of Susan's career can be seen as an act of kindness, as well as of defiance; and his belief in her talents is not in doubt. He is not intrinsically evil; his riches finish the work begun by his bank schooling.

The portrait is a generous one; but it is not altogether in the round: it is a brilliant sketch with the defects and virtues mapped by dashing strokes, yet the essence of the man is not quite there. We know, despite all the commentaries, too little about Kane: and here we see the limitations of the film. Kane's conversation almost throughout is staccato, a series of shouts across echoing rooms, mere illustrative noises in a void. We see only a dazzlingly illuminated cartoon figure, as two-dimensional as Colonel Blimp. The other characters are even more caricatured, made to live by performance rather than by the writing. Kane's parents are just a taut, nervous woman and an irascible old man in the script; Kane's mother, though, is brought to life by Agnes Moorehead as vividly as any crofter in *Man of Aran,* so that we see a lifetime of drudgery reflected in the shiny cheekbones, the tight mouth of the hoarder of cash. Thatcher, the great New York banker, is made to seem in George Coulouris's clever but hammy performance a stuffed shirt, an overbearing, crude, foolish figure of fun—even, oddly, in his own eyes when he is narrator through the pages of his diary.

Bernstein, the editor, is a faithful lapdog, sycophantic, silly, and finally a tired old man talking nostalgically about a girl he saw on a ferry. Leland is at best a genial stuffed shirt, at worst a pompous fool who declines into pathetic senility, trying to sneak cigars past the nurses in a hospital. Susan—beautifully played by Dorothy Comingore—is, like Kane's dull and genteel first wife, a disagreeable character, who fails to enlist our sympathy: at first a mindless girl, then later a loud-mouthed and vulgar middle-aged woman whose screeching is parodied in the image of a white cockatoo, flapping and crying as she walks out of Xanadu for the last time.

Dickens in his humorous mood sets the tone of all these characterizations, as well as that of much of the pace of the first half of the film, with its boisterous allegro clip, its procession of grotesques wonderfully observed in graphically compact images of greed, lust, and humor, marred only by the occasional ponderous writing.

The second half is taken at an altogether slower pace, a long *andante* in keeping with Kane's declining years and the somber setting of Xanadu. The film goes beautifully in these quieter passages: the last scenes with Thatcher, the still, poised sequence shot against rainswept windows in Bernstein's editorial office.

But despite such simple moments when the film seems to go deeper, into a more poetic and evocative mood, it is for the most part a display of epic journalism, its flair expressed in vivid evocations of successive periods from the stuffy nineteenth-century interiors of Kane's pre-Xanadu house to the tawdry worthlessness of Susan's nightclub.

Kane is a work of confidence and excess, as bold as a fresco, and it reminds one again that the cinema has continued a nineteenth-century fiction tradition of size and grandeur when the novel (in English at least) has largely shrunk to the trivial. It is the story of a man haunted for a lifetime by the memory of the purity of a childhood of poverty, frustrated at being raised by a bank, stripped of a normal boyhood, and given only the severe tutelage of the commercial East. Yet it is a film obsessed by the material splendor it attempts to deride, as are almost all Welles's films. The uses of the image of the sled and the snow symbols of "innocence" indicate Welles's profoundly American nostalgic romanticism; he cannot shake off the myth of the beauty of youth, or of an America that no longer exists, that perhaps never existed except in the imagination: the snow scenes when Charles is separated from his parents have all the concentrated frosty nostalgia of a *New Yorker* poem or winter short story.[6]

Yet if much of the film reflects a sentimental romanticism, its structure is cynical. This cynicism lies in the technique of having people comment on Kane who are themselves comically overdrawn witnesses to a serious career. If we cannot take them seriously, we cannot take their views seriously; and if Kane emerges from their accounts making any sense at all, it is in spite of them.

The film displays a split personality: on the one hand attracted to

[6] The Australian magazine *People* reported in its issue for January 30, 1952: "Residents in Stockholm were shocked in January of 1950 to see Welles rolling in the snow that blanketed one of their most fashionable streets. He was snorting and laughing happily. He got up, shook his snow encrusted body and said in his famous voice: 'I've wanted to do this since I was a little boy.'"

splendor, on the other attracted to deprivation. Kane says that if he had had no money, he would have been great; Welles is saying that Kane's fabulous acquisitions mean nothing, that all they symbolize in the end is the broken jigsaw puzzle of emotional ruin that dissolves into the smoke rising sluggishly from the chimney of Xanadu. Yet if this is a film that seems to criticize the heartless acquisition of riches, it reflects its creator's almost lascivious dwelling on the appurtenances of riches as well.

If *Citizen Kane*'s basic mood is anti-American, or at least anti-Middle West, it is also a wholly American work in its energy, opulence, ambition, and drive. It takes in a range of types, which, though Dickensian, are also of the America of cinema, comic strips, and radio: from the crumbling Bernstein to the hysterical caricature of the singing Matiste. It moves across an American scene from the timeless, antique-laden world of the Florida castle to the El Rancho nightclub, from the drab offices of *The Inquirer* where Jedediah Leland makes his career to the silent hospital where he ends his days. Welles takes in vivid fragments of a society, if not the whole of a man—and all in a series of searchlight glimpses, reminding us as well of mortality, looking hard at the face of old age, of dissolution. Xanadu becomes a tomb as much as the El Rancho: a tomb for lost American ambitions, for a childhood dream of hope at the turn of the century, buried somewhere deep in the material splendor of 1940.

Letter of Clearance from the Production Code Office[1]

◈◈◈

COPIES TO: MR. EDINGTON MR. HASTINGS
　　　　　　MR. WELLES (3) MR. McDONOUGH
　　　　　　　　　　　　　　MR. CRONE (2)
FROM: COLLIER YOUNG MR. WILKINSON

July 15, 1940

Mr. Joseph J. Nolan
RKO-Radio Pictures, Inc.
780 North Gower Street
Hollywood, California

Dear Mr. Nolan:

　We have read the second revised final script, dated July 9th, 1940, for your proposed production, titled CITIZEN KANE, and we are pleased to advise you that the material, except as noted hereinafter, is acceptable under the provisions of the Production Code and suggests no danger from the standpoint of political censorship.

There is one important detail in the story at hand, which is quite definitely in violation of the Production Code and, consequently, cannot be approved. This is the locale, set down for scene C, which is, inescapably, a brothel. Please have it in mind that there is a specific regulation in the Production Code, which prohibits the exhibition of brothels.

In all the circumstances, we suggest that the locale in this scene be changed and that there be nothing about the playing of the scene which would suggest that the place is a brothel.

Going through the script, page by page, we respectfully direct your attention to the following details:

Scenes 17, *et seq*.: Here and elsewhere, it will be necessary that you hold to an *absolute minimum* all scenes of drinking and drunkenness, wherever these occur. Have in mind that such scenes are acceptable only when they are necessary "for characterization or proper plot motivation."

Page 83: There should be nothing about this scene which indicates that Georgio is a "madam" or that the girls brought into the party are prostitutes. This flavor should be very carefully guarded against.

Page 119: Please eliminate the word "Lord" from Kane's speech, ". . . the Lord only knows . . ."

Page 152: The Action of the Assistant "patting the statue on the fanny," should be eliminated.

You understand, of course, that our final judgment will be based upon our review of the finished picture.

Cordially yours,
JOSEPH I. BREEN

CC. Mr. Wilkinson
Mr. Young

Printed by permission of the Motion Picture Association of America, Inc.

[1] This letter suggests that an earlier version of the script was different in some significant details from the three preserved at the Museum of Modern Art and reveals the general climate within which films were made in pre-World War II Hollywood.

Plot Synopsis

Charles Foster Kane dies at the age of seventy-six in his immense castle, Xanadu; his dying word is "Rosebud." In the projection room of a newsreel firm, a group of reporters note that Kane's public life—wealth, political and social events—does not contain the answer to the enigmatic "Rosebud." A reporter sets out to find the solution and, after reading the details of Kane's ruptured childhood, interviews four leading figures in the magnate's life: Bernstein, Leland (both associates of Kane at the height of his fame); his second wife, Susan Alexander, who Kane had forced to become an opera singer against her will and who is now drunk in a dingy nightclub; and Raymond, Kane's butler in the concluding stages of his life at Xanadu. All these are most forthcoming; some even give different versions of the same events; but none can explain the word "Rosebud" to Thompson, the reporter. The answer is given to the audience at the end: as Kane's belongings are packed up and removed from Xanadu, a workman tosses an old sledge into a fire. Painted on it is the word "Rosebud." It is the dim memory of his childhood toy that has haunted Kane throughout his life and on his deathbed.

This synopsis precedes the analysis of Kane *in Peter Cowie,* The Cinema of Orson Welles *(1965), pp. 21–22.*

III. Thompson Visits Susan Alexander Kane

Long tracking shot in rain over roof and through skylight of Susan's cabaret.
Susan refuses to talk, orders Thompson out.
Thompson calls Rawlston from pay phone.
Thompson's conversation with waiter: "She never heard of 'Rosebud.'"

IV. Thompson's Visit to Thatcher Library

Conversation with officious librarian and guard.
In the library vault with memoirs.

Young Kane in snow with sled.
Interior of house: Thatcher with Mr. and Mrs. Kane. Outside young Kane is seen throwing snowballs and heard shouting, "The Union Forever."
First encounter between Thatcher and young Kane outside house; parents tell boy he must go with Thatcher.
Shot of sled in falling snow dissolves to fancy new sled.

Rapid sequence of shots develop Thatcher-Kane relationship with skillful transitions both visual and aural.
Thatcher, Kane, and Bernstein in office as Kane signs over control of his enterprises in 1929. Kane: "If I hadn't been very rich I might have been a really great man."
Final shot in Thatcher Library.

V. Thompson and Bernstein

Bernstein and Thompson talk as rain beats on window; Bernstein tells story of girl in white dress.
Establishment of *Inquirer*.
   First day at the office.
   Kane and old editor, Carter.
   Story of missing women from Brooklyn.
   Kane's "Declaration of Principles," original of which Leland asks to keep.
The Rise of the *Inquirer*.
Party celebrating ascendency of *Inquirer* over *Chronicle*.

In rapid sequence:
> Photograph of former *Chronicle* staff changes to present *Inquirer* staff, Kane as master of ceremonies, band and girls enter, Bernstein and Leland talk as Kane dances.

Kane's trip to Europe.
Montage of collections he ships back.
Kane's return, presentation of cup, announcement of marriage to Emily Norton.

Back to Bernstein's office. Bernstein: "He was a man who lost almost everything he had."

VI. THOMPSON AND LELAND

Shot of bridge.
Leland in hospital.

Kane and Emily; the disintegration of their marriage.
Back to hospital.
Kane's meeting with Susan Alexander.
> Amuses Susan by wiggling his ears, making shadow figures (last of rooster), exchanging confidences; she sings and he applauds.

Political campaign.
> Leland's speech.
> Kane in huge hall speaking in front of poster.
> Shots of family and then Gettys as he leaves.
> Speech ends and Kane and Emily meet at car.

"Lovenest" sequence.
> Through door, upstairs, confrontation of Emily, Susan, Gettys, and Kane which ends with Kane vowing to send Gettys to Sing Sing and stiffly polite going of their separate ways by Gettys and Emily.

Campaign ends, Bernstein selects headline: "FRAUD AT THE POLLS"
Campaign Headquarters and confrontation between Kane and Leland.
> Leland: "You want love on your own terms." Kane: "Those are the only ones anyone ever knows—his own."

Marriage of Kane and Susan.

First opera sequence.
Ends with stagehand in flies holding his nose.

Chicago *Inquirer* office after performance.
Leland in drunken sleep at typewriter.
Kane and Bernstein enter; Bernstein reads unfinished notice in typewriter; Kane snatches it away to finish it.
Leland awakes, goes to where Kane is typing, and is fired by Kane.

Return to hospital.
Final comments on Kane.
Leland, asking Thompson again for cigars, is led away by nurses.

VII. THOMPSON AND SUSAN ALEXANDER KANE

Shot over cabaret roof as in earlier sequence.
Thompson and Susan at table.
Susan: "Everything was his idea."
Singing lesson: Susan, Matisti, Kane.
Opera House sequence (as experienced by Susan).
　Reactions of Leland, Bernstein, etc. culminating in Kane's solitary applause.

Susan and Kane the morning after debut.
Susan screams about Leland's bad review; messenger arrives with torn-up check and original copy of "Declaration of Principles."
Argue about Susan's future.

Montage of her disasterous singing career ending with visual and aural "running-down."

Susan's bedroom (and deep-focus shot of glass, bed, door): Susan has attempted suicide and Kane finally agrees to let her withdraw from operatic career.

Susan and Kane at Xanadu.
　Susan doing crossword puzzle.
　Susan's desire to go to New York.
　Kane (as he moves to fireplace): "Our home is here."
　Crossword puzzles suggest tedium and passing of seasons.
　Talk across huge room—cars along beach, cut to—

Content Outline 153

Picnic at Xanadu.
   Old Negro singer: "It can't be love."
   Kane and Susan argue, he slaps her.

Susan packs and leaves.
Back to cabaret; Susan suggests Thompson interview Raymond, the butler.

VIII. THOMPSON AND RAYMOND

Raymond lights cigarette, asks how much meaning of "Rosebud" is worth.

Raymond's version of Susan's departure.
   Kane wrecks Susan's room, picks up paperweight, says "Rosebud" and walks slowly past servants and in front of infinitely reflecting mirrors.

Back to Raymond: Thompson tells him the information not worth $1000.

IX. FINALE

Thompson descends stairs.
Tracking shot through hall and over Kane's collections, statues, memorabilia.

Thompson and photographers in shadows as Thompson reflects on his failure to find "Rosebud." Thompson: "Something he couldn't get or something he lost."

Reporters leave.
Long tracking shot over sea-like expanse of crates, boxes, etc. to furnace.
Shot of "Rosebud" being consumed in furnace.
Shots of Xanadu and fences, reversing those in Introduction.
Long shot of Xanadu and smoke.
"No Trespassing."

Script Extract

LENGTH	SCENE		REEL 5
FT. FRM.	NO.		SEC. 5A

[Scene 1: discussion between Kane and Leland; scene 2: Kane and reporters following wedding.]

5-5 3. INSERT #2—sign reading—music playing—
    KANE BUILDS
    OPERA HOUSE

Lap Dissolve

37-15 4. INT. ROOM CU—Susan with mouth open, singing Aria—tears in eyes—she turns as director comes on at right, raving—waving hands—

Director

No, no, no, no, no, no . . .
he talks indistinctly as camera moves back—hands at left putting plumed cap on Susan's head—much yelling and confusion—camera pans up to spotlight blinking—music—camera pans back down to Susan with people around her—adjusting her costume—director raving indistinctly—others wringing their hands—more people coming on—camera moving back—general confusion—

83-11 5. INT. STAGE LS—Susan in center—others around her—stagehands moving around with equipment—general excitement—music playing loudly—people rushing around—man waves, calls—

Man

Places, please.

helpers rush off stage—spotlight rises, exits—Susan posing—curtain goes up, showing stage—Susan sings—

Susan

Ah, cruel . .

Extract from Citizen Kane *cutting continuity script by Herman J. Mankiewicz and Orson Welles, copyright © 1971 by Bantam Books, Inc. The entire script will appear in Pauline Kael,* The Citizen Kane Book *(Boston: Little, Brown and Company, 1971). Reprinted by permission of Bantam Books, Inc.*

| LENGTH | SCENE | | REEL 5 |
| FT. FRM. | NO. | | SEC. 5A |

    camera moves upward—Susan and others exit—camera moving up over top of set—

Susan-off

    Tu mas trop entendus . .

    camera moving up to top of set—Susan heard singing indistinctly—camera stops on two men up on catwalk—looking down—one puts fingers to nose, holding his nose—

    Lap Dissolve

26-   6.   INT. OFFICE MS—Shadow of Kane comes on outside—comes into room—moves slowly to fg, listening—

Bernstein

Mr. Leland is writing it from the dramatic angle?

Editor-off

Yes.

Eddie-off

And we've covered it from the news end.

Editor-off

Naturally.

Bernstein-off

And the social. How about the music notice? You got that in?

Editor-off

Oh, yes, it's already made up.

124-12   7.   INT. OFFICE LS—Bernstein and men talking—Kane by doors in bg—

Editor

Our Mr. Mervin wrote a swell review.

Bernstein

Enthusiastic?

Mervin

Yes, sir.

Editor

Naturally.

Kane

Mr. Bernstein . .

group turning—men talking as Kane comes to them—

Mervin

Mr. Kane.

SCRIPT EXTRACT

LENGTH SCENE   REEL 5
FT. FRM. NO.   SEC. 5A

Bernstein
Hello, Mr. Kane.

Kane
Gentlemen.

Editor
Mr. Kane, this is a surprise.

Eddie
Hello, Mr. Kane, everything has been done exactly to your instructions.

Kane
Got a nice plant here.

Editor
We've got two spreads of pictures.

Kane
Fine. The music notice on the front page?

Mervin
Yes, Mr. Kane.

Editor
But there's still one notice to come. The dramatic.

Kane
The dramatic notice. Mr. Bernstein, that's Mr. Leland, isn't it?

Bernstein
Yes, Mr. Kane, we're waiting for it!

Kane
Where is he?

Mervin
Right in there, Mr. Kane.

Kane crosses to right—camera swings around—others exit—he goes down thru office to bg—two men working in bg—

Bernstein-off
Mr. Kane ..

Kane continues to bg—Bernstein coming on in fg—

Bernstein
.. Mr. Kane ..

Kane goes into office in bg, exits—Bernstein turns—man coming partly on at left fg—

| LENGTH | SCENE | | REEL 5 |
| FT. FRM. | NO. | | SEC. 5A |

> *Bernstein*
> Mr. Leland and Mr. Kane, haven't spoken together for years.

another man comes on—

> *Eddie*
> You don't suppose . . .

> *Bernstein*
> There's nothing to suppose. Excuse me.

Bernstein hurries into office in bg—

16-8   8. INT. ROOM CS—camera shooting up over desk—Leland asleep—head on typewriter in fg—bottle and glass by him—Bernstein coming in doorway in bg—stops—comes to desk—shakes Leland—looks up worried—

8-9   9. INT. OFFICE MCS—Bernstein right fg behind Leland asleep on desk—Kane in bg on other side—Bernstein turns, exits—

10-10 10. INT. OFFICE CS—camera shooting over desk—Leland asleep on typewriter in fg—Bernstein turning by door in bg talking—coming back to fg—

> *Bernstein*
> He ain't been drinking before, Mr. Kane. Never. We would have heard.

> *Kane-off*
> What does it say there?

6-2   11. INT. OFFICE MCS—Bernstein at right fg behind Leland lying on typewriter—Kane standing on other side of desk—talks—

> *Kane*
> The notice . . what's he written?

Bernstein looks around—

35-3   12. INT. OFFICE CS—Leland asleep on typewriter at right—Bernstein by him—looks at paper in typewriter, talks—

> *Bernstein*
> Miss Susan Alexander, a pretty but hopelessly incompetent amateur . .

he reads hesitatingly—

> *Bernstein*
> . . last night opened the new Chicago Opera House in a performance of . . . I still can't pronounce that name, Mr. Kane . .

34-13 13. INT. OFFICE MCS—Bernstein leaning over, looking at paper in typewriter—Leland with head on it—Kane standing on other side—

LENGTH	SCENE		REEL 5
FT. FRM.	NO.		SEC. 5A

Bernstein
Her singing, happily, is no concern of this department. Of her acting, it is absolutely impossible to . .

Kane
Go on.

Bernstein
That's all there is . .

Kane reaches toward typewriter—

5-5   14.   INT. OFFICE CS—Leland asleep on typewriter—Bernstein standing at left—Kane's hand coming on in fg—rips paper from typewriter—exits—

19-7   15.   INT. OFFICE MCS—Leland asleep on typewriter—Bernstein at right near fg—leaning over—Kane on other side of desk laughing—talks—

Kane
Of her acting it is absolutely impossible to say anything except that in the opinion of this reviewer it represents a new low. Have you got that, Mr. Bernstein?

3-6   16.   INT. OFFICE CS—Leland asleep on typewriter—Bernstein looking to fg—

Kane-off
In the opinion of this reviewer . .

Bernstein
I didn't see that.

2-11   17.   INT. OFFICE MCS—Bernstein at right of Leland—Kane standing in bg talking—

Kane
It isn't here, Mr. Bernstein, I'm dictating it.

5-5   18.   INT. OFFICE CS—Leland on typewriter—Bernstein at left talks—

Bernstein
But Mr. Kane, I . .

Kane-off
Get me a typewriter.

7-13   19.   INT. OFFICE MCS—Bernstein at right of Leland asleep on typewriter—Kane in bg talking, smiling—

Kane
I'm going to finish Mr. Leland's notice.

Lap Dissolve

5-4   20.   INSERT #3—Keys hitting paper in typewriter—spelling word W E A K—

Lap Dissolve

LENGTH	SCENE		REEL 5
FT. FRM.	NO.		SEC. 5A
66-	21.	INT. OFFICE CS—Leland with head on typewriter—sits up blinking—bottle and glass by him—he looks around—puts cigar to mouth—looks to fg—Bernstein comes on left fg with match—lights cigar—	

       Leland
  Hello, Bernstein. Hello.

       Bernstein
  Hello, Mr. Leland.

Leland chuckles—looking around—

       Leland
  Where's my notice, Bernstein? I've got to finish my notice.

       Bernstein
  Mr. Kane is finishing it for you.

       Leland
  Charlie?

they look at door in bg—Leland rising—

       Leland
  Charlie . . Charlie . . out there?

Leland goes to door in bg—Bernstein leans back, exits—

       Leland
  Huh, I guess he's fixing it up.

| 40-3 | 22. | INT. OFFICE CS—camera shooting up to Leland turning to fg—talking— |

       Leland
  I knew I'd never get that thru.

Bernstein comes on at left—

       Bernstein
  Mr. Kane is finishing your review just the way you started it. He's writing a bad notice like you wanted it to be. I guess that'll show you.

Leland turns—goes thru doorway into room in bg—

| 58-5 | 23. | INT. OFFICE LS—Kane partly on right fg typing—Leland coming from office in far bg—comes to fg—Bernstein in doorway in bg—Leland stops by railing at right—Kane glances up, talks— |

       Kane
  Hello, Jedediah.

       Leland
  Hello, Charlie, I didn't know we were speaking.

SCRIPT EXTRACT

LENGTH SCENE
FT. FRM. NO.

REEL 5
SEC. 5A

>Kane
>Sure we're speaking, Jedediah. You're fired.

he swings carriage back—types—Leland staring at him—

END OF REEL 5
SECTION 5A

REEL 5

SECTION 5B

Night Sequence

21-10 1. INT. ROOM CU—Leland's face before camera—he turns to right bg—typewriter heard—music playing—

he goes to bg—

Lap Dissolve

195- 2. (*Split screen shot*)

EXT. ROOF CS—Leland sitting at left below camera—scene of editorial room at right showing Kane sitting typewriting—Bernstein in doorway in far bg—watching—

>*Thompson-off*
>Everybody knows that story, Mr. Leland, but why did he do it?

scene of Kane in office exits—light shining down on Leland—

>*Thompson-off*
>How could a man write a notice like that when . .

Leland smiles—

>*Leland*
>You just don't know Charlie. He thought that by finishing that notice he could show me he was an honest man. He was always trying to prove something. That whole thing about Susie being an opera singer, that was trying to prove something.

he leans forward, laughing—camera moves back slightly showing Thompson partly on below at right fg—

>*Leland*
>You know what the headline was the day before the election? Candidate Kane Found In Love Nest With quote Singer unquote. He was going to take the quotes off the singer.

he calls to bg—

LENGTH	SCENE		REEL 5
FT. FRM.	NO.		SEC. 5A

Leland

Hey, nurse!

he talks to Thompson—

Leland

Five years ago he wrote from that place of his down south, you know, Shangri-la? El Dorado? Sloppy Joe's? What's the name of that place? All right, Xanadu. I knew what it was all the time. You caught on, didn't you? I guess maybe I'm not as hard to see thru as I think. Well, I never even answered his letter. Maybe I should have. I guess he was pretty lonely down there in that coliseum all those years. He hadn't finished it when she left him. He never finished it. He never finished anything, except my notice. Of course, he built the joint for her.

Thompson

That must have been love.

nurse comes on in bg—comes toward them, stops—

Leland

Oh, I don't know. He was disappointed in the world, so he built one of his own, an absolute monarchy. It was something bigger than an opera house, anyway.

he turns, calls—another nurse coming to fg—

Leland

Nurse.

Nurse

Yes, Mr. Leland.

Leland

Oh, I'm coming.

he leans toward Thompson—

Leland

Listen, young feller, there's one thing you can do for me.

Thompson

Sure.

Leland

Stop at the cigar store on your way out, will you and get me a couple of good cigars.

Thompson

I'll be glad to.

Leland

Thank you.

Leland rises—camera pans—Thompson rising at left fg—

SCRIPT EXTRACT

| LENGTH SCENE | REEL 5 |
| FT. FRM. NO. | SEC. 5A |

Leland

One is enough. You know, when I was a young man, there was an impression around that nurses were pretty. Well, it's no truer than it is today.

Nurse

I'll take your arm, Mr. Leland.

Leland

All right, all right. You won't forget about those cigars, will you?

Thompson

I won't.

Leland

And have them wrapped up to look like toothpaste, or something, or they'll stop them at the desk. You know, that young doctor, I was telling you about . . well, he's got an idea he wants to keep me alive.

nurses take Leland by arm—take him to bg—music playing—

Lap Dissolve

Day Sequence

25-7   3. EXT. BLDG, CU—picture of Susan—camera pans upward showing sign over bldg—

EL RANCHO
SUSAN ALEXANDER KANE

camera moves up to sign—passes thru it to skylight on top of bldg—

Lap Dissolve

103-8 4. INT. ROOM MCS—Thompson sitting at right fg, talks to Susan sitting at table, drinking—music—

Thompson

I'd rather you'd just talk. Anything that comes into your mind about yourself and Mr. Kane.

Susan puts glass down, simpering—

Susan

You wouldn't want to hear a lot of what comes into my mind about myself, and Mr. Charlie Kane. You know maybe I shouldn't have ever sung for Charlie the first time I met him, but I did an awful lot of singing after that. To start with, I sang for teachers at a hundred bucks an hour. The teachers got that. I . . .

Thompson

What did you get?

LENGTH SCENE
FT. FRM. NO.

REEL 5
SEC. 5A

Susan

I didn't get a thing except music lessons. That's all there was in it.

Thompson

He married you, didn't he?

Susan

He didn't mention anything about marriage until after it was all over, and until it got in the papers about it, and he lost the election, and that Norton woman divorced him. He was really interested in my voice. Why do you suppose he bought that opera house for? I didn't want it. I didn't want a thing. It was his idea. Everything was his idea, except my leaving him.

Lap Dissolve

Day Sequence

220-6 5. INT. ROOM LS—camera shooting down—Susan at right fg singing—pianist and Matisti sitting at piano—

Susan

Una voce poca fa
Quinel cor mi ri-sue-no
Il mio cor . .

Matisti rises, singing—camera moving around piano closer to them—

Matisti

Il mio cor . . don't forget . .
Ta-ta-ta, ta-ta-ta, ta-ta-ta, ta-ta-ta . .
Now, don't get nervous. Don't get nervous, please. Let's come back.
Da cappo . .

pianist plays—Matisti gesures, talks—Kane coming in doorway in bg—

Matisti

Look at me, Mrs. Kane . . darling . .

she sings—he talks in time with music—

Matisti

Now, get the voice out of the throat. Place the tone right in the mask—mmmmmm . . .

Susan-singing

Una voce poca fa
Quinel cor mi ri-sueno
Il mio cor-fe-ri-toe gia . . .

Matisti

Diaphram-a . . .

SCRIPT EXTRACT

LENGTH SCENE
FT. FRM. NO.

REEL 5
SEC. 5A

Susan-singing

E lindor fuche il piego
Si, lindo . . .

Susan stops, breaking on high note—he gestures wildly—sings→

Matisti

La-la-la-la . . you're out of pitch. La-la-la . .
Some people can sing. Some can't. Impossible. Impossible.

all look to bg as Kane in bg shouts at Matisti—coming toward them—

Kane

It is not your job to give your opinion of Mrs. Kane's talents. You're supposed to train her voice, Signor Matisti.

Matisti

Mr. Kane . .

Kane

Nothing more. Please sit down and continue with the lessons.

Matisti

But Mr. Kane . .

Kane

Please.

Kane stopping by them—

Matisti

But I will be the laughing stock of the musical world. The people will think . .

Kane

People will think. You're concerned about what people will think, Signor Matisti? I may be able to enlighten you a bit. I'm something of an authority about what people will think. The newspapers for example. I run several newspapers between here and San Francisco. It's all right, darling, Signor Matisti is going to listen to reason. Aren't you, Signor?

Matisti

How can I persuade you, Mr. Kane.

Kane

You can't.

Matisti turns mumbling, sits down by pianist—pianist plays—Susan sings—

Susan

Il mio cor fe-ri-oe gia
E Lindor fuche il piego
Si, Lindo . .

she looks down, ending on false note—others look down→

SCRIPT EXTRACT

LENGTH SCENE   REEL 5
FT. FRM. NO.   SEC. 5A

>   *Kane*
> It's all right, darling, go ahead.
>
> she sings—Kane smiling, talking to Matisti—
>
>   *Susan*
> Si, lindo-ro-mio-sa-ra
> Lo-gui-ra-i . .
>
>   *Kane*
> I thought you'd see it my way.
>
>   *Susan*
> . . la-vin-ce-ro
> E, Lindo . . ro-mio-sa-ra
> Lo gui-ra-i, la vin-ce-ro . .
>
>   Night Sequence

18-   6. INT. STAGE CU—Susan singing, tears in eyes—
>
>   *Susan*
> Ah, cruel . .
>
> Matisti comes on at right gesturing wildly—
>
>   *Matisti*
> No, no, no, no, no.
>
>   *Prompter*
> I should say not.
>
> others gathering around—
>
>   *Matisti*
> You must wait for the chord.
>
>   *Prompter*
> Wait for the chord.
>
>   *Maid*
> Miss Alexander . .
>
>   *Woman*
> Please . .
>
> man putting plummed hat on Susan—camera pans up to work light above—orchestra heard—
>
>   *Matisti-singing*
> One . . ah, cruel . . one . . ah cruel . .
> one . . ah, cruel . .

46-1   7. INT. STAGE LS—workmen and actors rushing around—Susan in center of stage—music heard—much confusion and yelling—light goes up—

Script Extract

| LENGTH
FT. FRM. | SCENE
NO. | | REEL 5
SEC. 5A |

people exit from stage—Susan posing—lights come on—curtains rise in bg, showing lights in audience—Susan sings—"SALAAMBO"—

(NOTE: Words of song and translation given at end of this reel. Song running thru scenes 8 to 30 inclusive)

7-   8. INT. THEATRE CU—Kane looking to fg—singing heard—

7-11   9. INT. THEATRE MLS—camera shooting past man's head in fg to Susan on stage in bg singing—people behind her—

7-13   10. INT. THEATRE CS—Leland looking at program—others partly on behind him—singing heard—

10-11   11. INT. STAGE LS—Susan by footlights, singing—lights seen in theatre in bg—

12-   12. INT. STAGE CS—Susan comes partly on at left, strutting—to left past lights—exits—Matisti and prompter in box in bg—singing heard—

3-3   13. INT. THEATRE CU—Matisti closes one eye, listening—singing heard—

11-6   14. INT. THEATRE MCS—Bernstein and men in box—others in bg—singing heard—

                                                                                                 Lap Dissolve

6-10   15. INT. STAGE MS—Susan singing—cast around her—

8-6   16. INT. THEATRE CU—man and Matisti looking to fg—Matisti motions, nodding—makes signs—singing heard—

7-1   17. INT. THEATRE MCU—Bernstein and man in fg—he nods—others in bg—singing heard—

7-9   18. INT. THEATRE CS—Leland tearing up program—others in bg—singing heard—

7-11   19. INT. THEATRE LS—camera shooting past Kane sitting partly on right fg—Susan on stage in bg singing—cast around her—

8-7   20. INT. THEATRE CU—Kane looking to fg—glances to right—singing heard—laughter and indistinct talking heard—

11-4   21. INT. STAGE CU—Susan singing—music heard—

7-15   22. INT. THEATRE CU—Kane looks forward grimly—singing, laughter and music heard—

9-9   23. INT. THEATRE MCU—Matisti behind lights—motions—hand to mouth—man at left by him—singing heard—

6-13   24. INT. THEATRE CS—Leland sitting with torn program—others behind—music and singing heard—

8-7   25. INT. THEATRE MCU—two behind lights—Matisti turning, waving arms—biting fingers—singing heard—

4-6   26. INT. THEATRE CS—Susan gesturing dramatically—singing—others in bg—

9-7   27. INT. THEATRE MCU—two behind lights—Matisti jumping up and down—whispers to man by him—singing and music heard—

LENGTH FT. FRM.	SCENE NO.		REEL 5 SEC. 5A

5-1   28. INT. THEATRE CU—Susan finishes singing—music—

3-14 29. INT. THEATRE CU—Kane looking to fg—singing heard—Susan holding note—music—

3-13 30. INT. THEATRE LS—camera shooting past Kane partly on left fg watching Susan and cast in bg on stage—Susan stops singing, sinks down dramatically—music—

7-1   31. INT. THEATRE CS—Leland tearing program in strips—music—others behind him, applaud slightly—

4-14 32. INT. THEATRE MCS—Bernstein and men in box applauding—light applause heard—people rising in bg—

[Words of song and translation omitted.]

END OF REEL 5
SECTION 5B

REEL 6

SECTION 6A

Night Sequence

11-13 1. INT. THEATRE CU—Kane seated in box, looking grimly to fg—applause heard—camera moves back showing others in box applauding—

3-4   2. INT. THEATRE MLS—camera shooting past Kane partly on at left fg looking down at stage—flowers below—light applause heard—

10-12 3. INT. THEATRE CU—Kane looking to fg—light applause heard—he glances around slightly—applauds—

3-7   4. INT. THEATRE MLS—camera shooting down to flowers on stage—Susan comes out from behind curtains right bg—applause heard—

4-10   5. INT. THEATRE CU—Kane applauding loudly—others heard applauding—

5-8   6. INT. THEATRE MLS—camera shooting down to Susan on stage—flowers around—others move up—

3-7   7. INT. THEATRE CU—Kane rising, applauding—camera tilts up, following him—

4-12   8. INT. THEATRE MLS—camera shooting down to Susan—flowers around—she backs away to right bg with rose—exits behind curtains—light applause heard—

17-   9. INT. THEATRE CU—camera shooting up to Kane applauding—light shines on him—he stops applauding—looks around—

Lap Dissolve

Filmography

For complete cast and production credits, shooting dates and locations, etc., the excellent filmographies of Welles in Peter Cowie's *The Cinema of Orson Welles* (London and New York, 1965), and in Charles Higham's *The Films of Orson Welles* (Berkeley, Los Angeles, and London, 1970) should be consulted. Cowie's book can also be consulted for information on Welles's acting roles on the stage and in film, his television and radio work, and his stage productions.

COMPLETED FILMS[1]

Citizen Kane, RKO-Radio Pictures. 1940–41.
The Magnificent Ambersons, RKO-Radio Pictures. 1942.
Journey into Fear, RKO-Radio Pictures. 1942–43.
The Stranger, International Production for RKO release. 1946.
The Lady from Shanghai, Columbia Pictures. 1947.
Macbeth, Charles K. Feldman for Republic Pictures. 1948.
Othello, Mercury Films. 1952.
Mr. Arkadin (or *Confidential Report*), Filmorsa. 1955.
Touch of Evil, Universal Pictures. 1957.
The Trial (or *Le Proces*), Mercury Production by Orson Welles, for Paris/Europa, FI-C-IT and HISA-Films. 1962.
Chimes at Midnight, International Films Española. 1965–66.

TELEVISION FILMS

The Fountain of Youth, Pilot for ABC, 1958.
Histoire Immortelle (The Immortal Story), ORTF-Albina Films, 1968.

---

[1] Welles also filmed sequences for stage productions for *Too Much Johnson, The Green Goddess, The Unthinking Lobster,* and *Around the World.* In addition he made a short film, *The Hearts of Age,* at the Todd School in 1934. For an analytic summary of this film see Joseph McBride, "Welles Before *Kane,*" *Film Quarterly* 23 (Spring 1970): 19–22. He may also have had some part in the filming of a Todd School production of *Twelfth Night.*

Uncompleted Films[2]

It's All True, RKO. 1941–42.
The Story of Jazz
My Friend Bonito
The Story of Samba, *The Samba Story*, or *Carnival*
Jangadeiros
Don Quixote
Dead Reckoning

[2] For a list—probably incomplete even as of 1965—of Welles's unrealized film projects see Peter Cowie's *The Cinema of Orson Welles* (1965).

Selected Bibliographies

The most complete listing (120 items) of writings by and about Orson Welles may be found in Peter Cowie, *The Cinema of Orson Welles* (London and New York, 1965), pp. 197–207. To this bibliography I have added below mainly items of special interest published since 1965 or items which do not appear on Cowie's list.

I. ORSON WELLES: BOOKS AND GENERAL STUDIES

Bogdanovich, Peter. *Conversations with Orson Welles.* Forthcoming, 1971.

———. "Is It True What They Say about Orson?" *The New York Times,* August 30, 1970, sec. 2, pp. 1–2. An attack on Charles Higham's *The Films of Orson Welles.* Attempts to correct what Bogdanovich sees as "destructive misrepresentations" of Welles's career, particularly as they suggest Welles has been profligate as a director and incapable of completing his work. See also Higham's response and Bogdanovich's reply in *The New York Times,* September 13, 1970, sec. 2.

*Cobos, Juan, Miguel Rubio, and José A. Pruneda. "A Trip to Don Quixoteland: Conversations with Orson Welles." *Cahiers du Cinéma* 165 (April 1965). Reprinted in English translation by Rose Kaplin in *Cahiers du Cinéma* (English) 5 (1966): 34–47. By far the richest printed interview with Welles to date.

Higham, Charles. *The Films of Orson Welles.* Berkeley, University of California Press, 1970.

*Johnson, William. "Orson Welles: Of Time and Loss." *Film Quarterly* 21 (1967): 13–24.

McBride, Joseph. His book on Welles will be published spring 1971 by Indiana University Press.

Tynan, Kenneth. "*Playboy* Interview: Orson Welles." *Playboy* 14

---

*Items marked with an asterisk are included in the text of this volume.

(March 1967): 53–54, 56, 58, 60, 62, 64. Some fresh biographical material and familiar opinions on other filmmakers.

II. ARTICLES, CHAPTERS AND REVIEWS ON *Citizen Kane*

Anonymous. "*Citizen Kane.*" *Documentary News Letter* 2 (November 1941): 215–16. Mixed review; makes curious claims concerning autobiographical elements in film.

*Belfrage, Cedric. "Orson Welles' *Citizen Kane.*" *The Clipper* 1 (May 1941). Reprinted in Lewis Jacobs, *Introduction to the Art of the Movies* (1960).

*Borges, Jorge Luis. "*Citizen Kane.*" *Sur* (Buenos Aires), No. 83 (1945). Reprinted in French translation in *Positif* 58 (February 1964): 17–18.

Bourgeois, Jacques. "Le Cinéma à la recherche du temps perdu," *La Revue du Cinéma* (Paris), December 1946. Proposes parallels between *Kane* and Proust's novel.

Cameron, Kate. "Review [of *Citizen Kane*]." *New York Daily News*, May 2, 1941, p. 4.

"*Citizen Kane.*" *Today's Cinema* 57 (October 7, 1941): 14.

"*Citizen Kane*: Twenty-Eight Years Later." *Montage* 3 (January–February 1970): 3–13. Brief essays by students in the Film Production Program at Northern Valley Regional High School, Demarest, New Jersey. (See Michael Stephanick, below).

*Cowie, Peter. *The Cinema of Orson Welles*. London and New York: Zwemmer and A. S. Barnes, 1965. Chapter 2, "The Study of a Colossus," which includes extracts from the screenplay, deals with *Kane*.

*Crowther, Bosley. ["A Review of *Citizen Kane.*"] *The New York Times*, May 2, 1941.

*———. "The Ambiguous Citizen Kane." *The New York Times*, May 4, 1941.

Cutts, John. "*Citizen Kane.*" *Films and Filming* 10 (December 1963): 15–19. An excellent summary survey of the film's subject and technique and its reception.

Domarchi, Jean. "America." *Cahiers du Cinéma*, 31 (November 1959): 51–55. Attempts to draw parallels between Kane and Welles.

*Ferguson, Otis. "Citizen Welles," *The New Republic* 114 (June 2, 1941): 760–61.

*Fowler, Roy A. *Orson Welles: A First Biography*. London: Pendulum Publications, 1946. Material on *Kane*, pp. 33–70.

*Herrmann, Bernard. "Score for a Film." *The New York Times*, May 25, 1941.
*Higham, Charles. See long chapter on *Kane* in book listed in section 1, excerpts from which appear in this volume, pp. 137–45.
Isaacs, Hermine Rich. "Citizen Kane and One-Man Pictures in General." *Theatre Arts* 25 (June 2, 1941): 427–34. Sees weakness of film in its being about "a man who is really not worth depicting," while acknowledging it has "the kind of artistic unity which is rare in Hollywood's customary large-scale collaborations."
Kael, Pauline. *The Citizen Kane Book*. Boston: Atlantic-Little, Brown, 1971, in press. The 50,000-word introduction is scheduled for separate publication in *The New Yorker*.
*Knight, Arthur, "*Citizen Kane* Revisited," *Action* 4 (1969): 33–35. See "Special Report . . ." below.
Kruk, Ewa. "*Citizen Kane*." *Filmcritica*, no. 188 (April 1968), pp. 217–29. Highly technical analysis.
*Lean, Tangye. "Pre-War Citizen." *Horizon* 4 (November 1941): 359–64.
"Le Dossier du Mois." *Cinema* (Paris), No. 96 (May 1965), pp. 46–53. Brief commentaries by Agel, Bazin, Bessy, Leenhardt, Mitry, Sadoul, and others, many of them unfavorable to Welles and *Kane*.
Leenhardt, Roger. "Citizen Kane." *Ecrans de France* (Paris), July 3, 1946.
Lopiensk, B. "Citizen Kane." *Filmcritica*, no. 179–80 (August 1967), pp. 356–70. Highly technical analysis.
McBride, Joseph. "*Citizen Kane*." *Film Heritage* 4 (Fall 1968): 7–18. Maintains that time is the protagonist of *Kane*. An expanded and revised version of this essay will appear in McBride's Cinema One series book on Welles, scheduled for spring 1971 by Indiana University Press.
*O'Hara, John. "*Citizen Kane*." *Newsweek* 13 (March 17, 1941): 60.
Rispoli, Claudiao. *Filmcritica*, no. 147–48 (July–August 1964), pp. 373–80.
Rotha, Paul. *The Film Till Now*. London: Spring Books, 1967. Pages 495–97 offer a sharply critical appraisal. "Most of his methods are crude and eclectic adaptations. . . ."
*Sarris, Andrew. "*Citizen Kane*: The American Baroque." *Film Culture* 2 (1956): 14–16.
Sartre, Jean-Paul. "When Hollywood Wants to Make Itself Think." *L'Ecran Francais* (Paris), August 1, 1945. Notable for its irrelevant observations about Welles's failure to be in touch with the masses.

Sheridan, M. C., H. H. Owen, Jr., K. Macrorie, and F. Marcus. *The Motion Picture and the Teaching of English.* New York: Appleton-Century-Crofts, 1965. Chapter 6, "Analysis of a Film Classic," is devoted to a sensible discussion of *Kane.*

"Special Report: *Citizen Kane* Remembered," *Action* 4 (1969): 24–35. Brief recollections by John Houseman, Richard Wilson, William Alland, Ralph Hoge, Paul Stewart, Agnes Moorehead, Joseph Cotten, James Stewart, Robert Wise, Mark Robson. Separate essay by Arthur Knight, "*Citizen Kane* Revisited," pp. 33–35.

*Stephanick, Michael. "The Most Advanced Film Screened in Class This Year: A Catalogue of Effects." *Montage* 3 (January–February 1970): 5–7. See "*Citizen Kane*: Twenty-Eight Years Later," above.

*Toland, Gregg. "I Broke the Rules in *Citizen Kane*," *Popular Photography* 8 (June 1941): 55.

*Truffaut, François. "*Citizen Kane.*" *L'Express* (Paris), November 26, 1959.

*Welles, Orson. "*Citizen Kane* Is Not About Louella Parsons' Boss." *Friday* 2 (February 14, 1941): 9.

Index[1]

Aeschylus, 114
À la Recherche du Temps Perdu, 62
Aldrich, Robert, 22
Alexander, Susan (typist), 139
Alexander, Susan (*see* Kane, Mrs. Susan Alexander)
All the King's Men, 109
Anderson, Maxwell, 87
Anderson, Sherwood, 87
Arliss, George, 61
Asphalt Jungle, The, 22

Bacall, Lauren, 130
Badge of Evil, 31
Barnes, Howard, 2
Barnum, P. T., 25, 26
Baxter, Keith, 32
Bazin, André, 2, 5, 109, 110, 111, 113, 116
Beckett, Samuel, 12
Belfrage, Cedric, 3
Benét, Stephen Vincent, 87
Bergman, Ingmar, 109
Bergman, Ingrid, 130
Bernstein, Doctor, 110
Bernstein, Mr., 27, 63, 98, 110, 111, 115, 118, 135, 136, 140, 142, 143, 144, 145
Bessy, Maurice, 2, 110
Big Parade, The, 46
Big Sleep, The, 37
Billetdoux, 131
Birth of a Nation, The, 46, 88
Bitsch, Charles, 109
Bitzer, Billy, 51
Blackmail, 131
Blake, Nicholas (Cecil Day Lewis), 80
Blitzstein, Marc, 121
Bogart, Humphrey, 130
Bonaparte, Napoleon, 61
Borges, Jorge Luis, 1, 5

Boudu Sauvé des Eaux, 114
Bourgeois, Jacques, 114
Boyd, James, 87
Brecht, Bertold, 14
Bridges, Harry, 100
Brisbane, Arthur, 140
Brulatour, Jules, 113
Buñuel, Luis, 117

Cabinet des Dr. Caligari, Das, 99
Cabinet of Dr. Caligari, The, 120
Cameron, Kate, 2
Carné, Marcel, 118
Carter, 119
Carvalho, S. S., 140
Casino Royale, 26
Cezanne, Paul, 12
Chance, 127
Chaplin, Charles, 56, 58, 88, 98, 130
Chesterton, G. K., 127
Chicago American, 139
Chin Chin, 131
Chronicle, The, 116, 122
"The Citizen," 127
Citizen Hearst, 140
Cobos, Juan, 3
Cocteau, Jean, 2
Collins, Ray, 53, 87, 95, 98, 134
Comingore, Dorothy, 51, 53, 98, 107, 143
Confidential Report, 119, 133
Connelly, Marc, 87
Conrad, Joseph, 5, 6, 79, 80, 127
Cooper, Gary, 130
Cotten, Joseph, 27, 51, 53, 98, 107, 119
Coulouris, George, 98, 143
Cowie, Peter, 4
Cradle Will Rock, The, 121
Creelman, Eileen, 100
Crime and Punishment, 13, 14
Crowther, Bosley, 2, 3, 100

---

[1] Index covers pp. 1–145 only and excludes references to Charles Foster Kane, *Citizen Kane,* and Orson Welles.

Dali, Salvador, 36
d'Annunzio, Gabriele, 19
Davies, Marion, 113, 138
del Rio, Dolores, 83, 86, 100
de Rochemont, Louis, 97
Detroit Times, 83
Dickens, Charles, 144
Documentary News Letter, 2
Domarchi, Jean, 109
Dos Passos, John, 113
Dostoievsky, Feodor, 12, 13
Drake, Herbert, 79, 80, 86

Eisenstein, Sergei, 9
Ermolieff, Joseph N., 84

Face in the Crowd, A, 109
Fahrenheit 451, 36
Falstaff, 19, 20, 25, 28, 29, 31, 33, 37
Ferguson, Otis, 2, 3
Fernandez, Macedono, 127
Feuillere, Edwige, 130
Films of Orson Welles, The, 4
Fitzgerald, F. Scott, 6, 46
Five Kings, 84
Ford, Ford Maddox, 5, 6
Ford, John, 6, 9, 11, 112, 120
Forerunners of American Fascism, 140
Foster, Norman, 25
Fowler, Roy A., 4
Fresnay, Pierre, 130
Freud, Sigmund, 2, 28, 63
Friday, 67, 68
Furie, Sidney J., 40

Galileo Galilei, 14
Gettys, James W. ("Boss"), 6, 30, 91, 94, 98, 110, 122, 123, 135, 140, 142
Gielgud, John, 32
Godard, Jean-Luc, 40
Goldwyn, Samuel, 82
Goya, Francisco, 12
Grande Illusion, La, 120
Grange, Fred, 138
Grant, Cary, 130
Grapes of Wrath, The, 6, 58, 76, 103, 120
Great Dictator, The, 102
Great Gatsby, The (film), 46
Green Hills of Africa, The, 17
Green, Paul, 87
Griffith, D. W., 9, 51, 88, 89, 114, 128
Group Theatre, 18
Guibert, Claire, 130

Hamlet, 59
Hawks, Howard, 12
Hays Office, 86
Head of Caesar, The, 127
Hearst, George, 138
Hearst, Phoebe, 139, 140
Hearst, William Randolph, 2, 4, 52, 57, 68, 81, 82, 83, 84, 85, 86, 87, 88, 100, 102, 103, 113, 137, 139, 140, 141
Heart of Darkness, 4, 5, 79, 80, 83
Hemingway, Ernest, 17, 131
Henry, O., 62
Henry V, 32
Henry IV, Parts I, II, 32
Henry IV, Part II, 29
Hernani, 64
Herrmann, Bernard, 4, 29, 48, 50, 121, 123, 139
Higham, Charles, 4, 5
His Honor, The Mayor, 87, 88
Hitchcock, Alfred, 22, 23, 34, 131, 132, 133
Hitler, Adolph, 141
Hopper, Hedda, 82, 83
Houseman, John, 23, 79, 80, 123
House on 92nd Street, The, 97
Hume, David, 127
Huston, John, 14, 15, 22

I Am a Fugitive from a Chain Gang, 123
Intolerance, 88, 89
Ionesco, Eugène, 12
I Was a Male War Bride, 12

Journey into Fear, 25
Johnson, William, 3
Joseph Conrad: A Personal Remembrance, 6
Jour Se Lève, Le, 118
Julius Caesar, 103, 121

Kafka, Franz, 13, 34, 38, 127
Kane, Mrs. Susan Alexander, 6, 25, 28, 30, 36, 60, 61, 63, 71, 90, 91, 92, 93, 94, 96, 97, 98, 110, 113, 116, 117, 118, 128, 134, 135, 139, 142, 143, 144
Kane, Mrs. Emily Norton, 112, 142
Kane, Mrs. (mother), 115
Kaplin, Rose, 7
Kazan, Elia, 109

INDEX

Killing, The, 22
King Lear, 102
Knight, Arthur, 4
Koheleth, 127
Kubrick, Stanley, 22

Lady from Shanghai, The, 10, 11, 25, 26, 28, 33, 37, 111, 131
L'Année dernière à Marienbad, 13
Last Year at Marienbad, 34
Lean, Tangye, 3
Leenhardt, Roger, 2
Left-Handed Gun, The, 22
Lejeune, C. A., 101
Leland, Jedediah, 28, 70, 90, 92, 93, 94, 97, 98, 110, 111, 115, 116, 117, 118, 123, 134, 135, 136, 137, 140, 142, 143, 145
Life, 78, 86
Lincoln, Abraham, 87
Lockhart, Gene, 79
Lombard, Carole, 81
Long Voyage Home, The, 76
Los Angeles Herald-Examiner, 85
Loyer, Raymond, 130
Lubitsch, Ernst, 22
Luce, Henry, 86, 90
Lupino, Ida, 130

M, 46
Macbeth, 26, 37, 39, 119, 121
McCarthy, Joseph (senator), 17
Mach, Ernest, 127
McKinley, William (president), 139
MacLeish, Archibald, 87
Magnificent Ambersons, The, 26, 27, 28, 29, 30, 32, 33, 37, 40, 92, 98, 122, 131, 132
Man of Aran, 143
Mankiewicz, Herman J., 5, 53, 81, 82, 89, 103, 109
Manon, 139
Marais, Jean, 130
Married Woman, The, 40
Marshall, Arthur Calder, 83
Marx, Karl, 63
Massenet, Jules, 139
Masterson, Whit, 31
Matisti, Signor, 94, 116, 145
Menjou, Adolph, 55
Mercury Players, 107
Mercury Theatre, 18, 55, 84, 85, 119, 123
Metropolis, 34
Miller, Arthur, 17

Milwaukee Sentinel, 84
Moby Dick, 14
Monroe, James (president), 139
Moorehead, Agnes, 95, 98, 119, 143
Moreau, Jeanne, 33
Morgan, J. P., 96, 140
Morgan, Michele, 130
Mortimer, Lee, 85
Motion Picture Herald, 81, 101
Mr. Arkadin, 11, 25, 26, 27, 30, 33, 38, 131
Murphy, Charles F., 140
Musketeers of Pig Alley, 114
Mussolini, Benito, 141
Myers, Gustavus, 52

Nabokov, Vladimir, 131
Naked Runner, The, 40
New Yorker, The, 131
New York Herald Tribune, 137
New York Inquirer, 70, 90, 92, 96, 116, 122, 134, 135, 139, 143, 145
New York Mirror, 85
New York Morning Journal, 139
New York Sun, 100
New York Times, 100
New York World, 139, 140
Neylan, John Francis, 140

Odlum, Floyd B., 86
Oh, Mr. Kane, 121
O'Hara, John, 3
Olivier, Laurence, 12
Othello, 33, 35, 37, 40, 119

Parlo, Dita, 80
Parsons, Louella, 1, 67, 68, 81, 82, 83
Penn, Arthur, 22
People, 144
Peran, Claude, 130
Powell, Dilys, 2, 113, 114, 123
Power and the Glory, The, 99, 127
Proust, Marcel, 60, 64, 131
Pruneda, J. A., 3
Pudovkin, Vsevolod, 128
Pulitzer, Joseph, 139
Purviance, Edna, 55

Ramsaye, Terry, 90, 91
Rawlston, 95
Ray, Nicholas, 22
Raymond, 91, 110, 117, 142
Règle du Jeu, La, 114
Reinhardt, Max, 78
Remington, Frederic, 139

Renoir, Jean, 9, 27, 114, 120, 130, 133
Rhinoceros, 12
Robinson, Edward G., 130
Robson, Mark, 123
Rope, 34
Rosebud, 2, 23, 27, 28, 35, 36, 48, 51, 56, 61, 62, 63, 70, 89, 92, 97, 103, 104, 105, 106, 108, 109, 110, 112, 115, 134, 135, 136, 138
Rossellini, Roberto, 133
Rossen, Robert, 109
Rubio, Miguel, 3
Russell, Rosalind, 81
Rutherford, Margaret, 34

Salammbo, 71, 118, 139
San Francisco Examiner, 139, 140
Sanderson, Sibyl, 139
Sanford, Erskine, 119
Sarnoff, David, 83
Saroyan, William, 87
Sarris, Andrew, 4
Sartre, Jean-Paul, 2
Schaefer, George J., 78, 82, 84, 85, 86
Schenck, Joseph, 83
Schenck, Nicholas, 83
Secret Life, 36
Seiderman, Maurice, 98
Shakespeare, William, 8, 13, 16, 26, 31, 32, 33, 35, 37
Sherwood, Robert W., 87
Sight and Sound, 16, 119, 120
Sleeping Beauty, The, 58
Sloane, E., 53, 98, 107, 119, 135
Smiler with a Knife, 4, 80
Soft Skin, The, 40
Stagecoach, 6, 112
Stalin, Joseph, 14
Stanislavski, Constantin, 14
Stein, Gertrude, 1
Stephanick, Michael, 5
Stewart, James, 130

Stranger, The, 26, 28, 37, 119
Sturges, Preston, 99
Swanberg, W. A., 140, 141
Swing, Raymond Gram, 140

Thaïs, 90, 139
Thatcher, Walter Parks, 89, 96, 98, 104, 110, 111, 112, 115, 117, 118, 119, 123, 134, 136, 140, 142, 143
Theatre Arts Monthly, 4
Third Man, The, 26
Thompson, 68, 89, 95, 118, 134
Tierney, Gene, 130
Time, 86, 90, 120
Tirez sur le Pianiste, 117
Toland, Gregg, 4, 23, 24, 47, 50, 53, 83, 92, 93, 95, 106, 114, 123
Tolstoy, Leo, 12
Touch of Evil, 19, 21, 25, 26, 28, 29, 30, 31, 33, 39, 40, 115, 119
Trial, The, 7, 13, 15, 25, 26, 28, 33, 34, 35, 38, 39, 40, 115
Truffaut, François, 2, 5, 36, 40, 117

Van Gogh, Vincent, 9
Van Schmus, 83
Variety, 85
Velasquez, Diego, 12, 13
Vlady, Marina, 33
Von Sternberg, Joseph, 22

Wages of Fear, The, 37
War of the Worlds, 121
Way to Santiago, The, 83
Weinberg, Herman G., 11
Whitebait, William, 2, 109
Wild Strawberries, 109
Wilson, Milicent, 139
Wise, Robert, 123
Wolfe, Thomas, 48
Wuthering Heights, 76
Wyler, William, 22, 23, 114